Wildflowers

of Newfoundland and Labrador

Peter J. Scott   Dorothy Black

Library and Archives Canada Cataloguing in Publication

Wildflowers of Newfoundland and Labrador / Peter J. Scott; illustrated by Dorothy Black

ISBN 978-0-9783381-6-9

1. Wildflowers-Newfoundland and Labrador-Identification.
I. Black, Dorothy II. Title.

QK203.N4S383 2006   582.1309718   C2006-901574-0

Printed and bound in China

Published by Boulder Publications
Portugal Cove-St. Philip's, Newfoundland & Labrador, Canada
www.boulderpublications.ca

Design and layout by Sarah Hansen

We acknowledge the financial support of the Government of Newfoundland and Labrador through the Department of Tourism, Culture and Recreation.

Dedications

By the artist: Dedicated with love to my husband, Douglas, who encouraged me. And, to my three children, Dori, Diane, and Don. If they complained of neglect during my five summers of work, I do not remember it. Also, in memory of my parents, who gave me arty genes and a love of flowers.

By the author: Dedicated to my parents, who encouraged and supported my love of plants and birds.

Contents

Artist's Preface

The flowers began it. Numerous, beautiful – they so delighted me that I wished to somehow capture their charms. Pressed and dried, they lost all beauty. Then my husband said, "You should be painting them!" And so, quite innocently – an amateur artist new to the watercolour medium and totally ignorant of botany – I set out to capture the wildflowers of Newfoundland and Labrador.

For five years this venture dominated our short summers. Holidays were spent touring the province in a camper van, which let us stop and stay wherever a new variety was discovered. Usually I would work from soon after daylight until dusk arrived. Then there was a relaxing search in the twilight for a new specimen to pick next morning. Darkness brought out the pile of newly acquired botany books wherein the new variety was, if possible, identified and studied so that no important characteristics would be missed in the painting. At the end of the summer the paintings and the dried specimens were passed on to Dr. Peter Scott at Memorial University for botanical inspection and identification.

These flower studies were done in drybrush watercolour. As each specimen was picked, it was measured carefully and painted in actual size. This presented certain problems such as how to adequately portray a large plant on such a small page, but paid dividends when the matter of publishing came up and all the paintings were the same convenient size. The flowers included here were chosen not necessarily for their beauty but often for characteristics of special interest and as representatives of plant families and habitats. To pick the branch or plant needed for each picture was painful, but hopefully justified by recording the flower in this way. I would have preferred to leave it in its natural setting to proliferate and give further joy to others.

This involvement with painting flowers was rewarding. The joys of expanding awareness, of sensing and learning, and finally creating, coloured my days. I cannot forget the thrills of first discovery, or finding in a plain, tiny flower a centre of immense and unexpected beauty. I can recall the rapture I experienced on beholding a green bank caught by the strong light of late day, studded with brilliantly glowing pitcher plants. Or, in early morning, the dew droplets scattered in profusion among the sunlit mosses of a bog. There were also frustrations, such as the flowers which drooped so quickly that they were difficult to paint, or those missed one summer for lack of time and lost the next to the 'progress' of a new road or town site. In a lighter vein, there was the frustration of carefully doing three Sedum rosea plants on the page and then being told they were all of the same sex, and would I paint another with both sexes! I often struggled to appear nonchalant and sane at moments when I felt otherwise. I tried not to dwell on what the inhabitants of one village must have thought the day we motored in, carefully dug up an immense and very spiny thistle, placed it in the car, and drove away.

That was 25 years ago. The book of wildflowers of Newfoundland and Labrador that was planned toward the end of those years of painting never materialized. In 1980 we left the province, and work on the collection came to an end.

One day in the spring of 2005, after being out of touch for many years, I received an e-mail from Dr. Scott asking if I still had the paintings. I did – they had spent those long years in my safe and had moved with us from Newfoundland to three different Ontario locations. To my great surprise, the reason for the e-mail was that it seemed we would finally be able to produce a book!

Here it is. The paintings of Newfoundland and Labrador wildflowers can now command a larger audience.

Author's Preface

It has been a real pleasure working with Dorothy on this book. She came to see me with her early works and we have proceeded from there to produce what you hold in your hands.

Dorothy's paintings are beautiful and the plants are artistically rendered. Two aspects of the paintings particularly appeal to me. One, they are faithful to the original plants. When Dorothy sent me batches of paintings for identification, I had no difficulty identifying the plants, as all of the necessary details of form were shown. Later in the season, when she sent the pressed specimens of the plants she painted, they always confirmed my identification. Two, all parts of the plant are given equal attention. It is a joy to see care and attention given to the bark, leaves, and stems as well as to the flowers.

The species included in this work were chosen on the basis of a number of criteria – wide distribution, a broad range of habitats, and/or interesting in some aspect of their biology.

Plant Family Names: I have used the traditional names of some families. Family names usually end in -aceae, but a few do not. These family names originated with early Greeks and celebrate a major feature of the group of plants. Cruciferae (Brassicaceae) refers to the cross shape of the four petals of the flower; Leguminosae (Fabaceae) refers to the legume fruit; Compositae (Asteraceae) refers to the composite flower; Labiatae (Lamiaceae) refers to the two lips of the flower; and Umbelliferae (Apiaceae) refers to the inflorescence (umbel). The species names of many North American plants have been revised in the past few years. I have only included the names used in commonly available manuals, rather than a list of synonyms for each plant, as this would be tedious for most readers.

The location where every plant was collected and painted is given below each description. The text has been written to complement the paintings. Please enjoy the book and then venture forth to see the originals.

Introduction

The flora of Newfoundland and Labrador is particularly fascinating, not because of its richness but because of its paucity and its odd assemblage of plants. Newfoundland pokes off the edge of the North American continent and gets the fringes of many different floras. Many plants reach the extreme of their range or ecological tolerance in Newfoundland. In addition, many plants do not fill the same ecological niche in this province that they do elsewhere. All of this leads to many delightful discoveries for anyone studying the flora. In Labrador the arctic flora reaches its southern limit and other floras extend into it.

The island of Newfoundland has an area of about 112,000 square kilometres. It is separated from Labrador by 18 kilometres and from Cape Breton Island by 114 kilometres. The island consists of a tilted plateau of moderate to slight relief and rises gradually to the west where there are elevations of about 760 metres. The entire island is quite hilly. Newfoundland has an interesting geological history, since the western part of the island is an extension of North America and the eastern portion was once part of northern Africa. When the two parts collided, there was an upwelling of magma, producing the mineral-rich deposits of central Newfoundland which have been mined. This geology leads to a difference in soils. The eastern portions of the island have acidic bedrock and glacial till derived from it which produce an acidic soil and, consequently, difficult growing conditions for plants. The western part of the island has calcareous soils, limestone outcrops, and cliffs, as well as several serpentine areas with a moonscape vegetation. Labrador, with an area of about 188,000 square kilometres, makes up the eastern half of the Ungava Peninsula, and is a tilted plateau which rises to the southwest. Labrador is the eastern portion of the Precambrian Canadian Shield.

The Vegetation
Labrador's flora is typical of its latitude, but Newfoundland's flora is an unusual mixture of plants with varied origins. A visitor to the island sees a Spruce/Balsam Fir forest of short stature, numerous peatlands, and headlands with short shrubs and herbs.

The flora is essentially boreal forest with these additional elements: 1) arctic species occur at higher elevations and on coastal cliffs, 2) some temperate-boreal species which grow on Cape Breton Island are absent on the island (e.g., the Eastern White Cedar and its associated species), 3) Coastal Plain species found from New Jersey northwards extend to the island and often grow in close association with arctic species, 4) some Cordilleran species, which have their main distribution in the mountains of western North America, are found on the mountains and unstable soils of western Newfoundland, 5) there are Amphiatlantic species that occur here and on the other side of the North Atlantic, and 6) many species have been introduced to the province by settlers.

Glaciation

The last glaciation scoured most of the island and Labrador. The soil was scraped off the island and deposited on the Grand Banks off the southeast coast of the island – this was good for the fish but not for the plants. The glaciers started to retreat about 13,000 years ago and the last of the ice melted off the island about 9,000 years ago and later from Labrador.

Recolonization

Plants likely recolonized via several routes. There is some evidence that a few of the higher hills on the west coast of the island and in Labrador were not glaciated and that some species survived there. It is thought that with a decrease in sea level during the glacial period some species remained on dry areas of the coast. A long stretch of land was exposed from just south of the Avalon Peninsula to New Jersey. Plants survived there and this land may have provided the avenue for the introduction of the Coastal Plain species. On the mainland, most of the vegetation retreated into the United States in front of the advancing ice sheet and then followed the ice back north into Labrador. Recolonization of the island involved a leap from southern Labrador onto the northern tip of the Northern Peninsula. Other species have arrived by the plethora of means used by plants.

Environmental Factors

Plant propagules often reach an area but may not become established. Newfoundland and Labrador have different environmental conditions which restrict some and allow other species to thrive.

Soil – Much of the province has shallow, stony, and acidic (typical pH range 4-4.4) soil and, since acidity interferes with nutrient availability, this restricts the growth of most plants. Some sites, for example, on the west coast of the island have calcareous or serpentine soils and this causes the greatest regional differences in the flora. Some southern species are restricted to these soils. Although most of the soil on the island is poor, pockets of fertile agricultural soil are scattered throughout (e.g., Codroy Valley, Cormack, Clarenville area, and parts of the Avalon Peninsula) and in Labrador (e.g., the shores of Lake Melville). Some areas in the central part of the island have sandy soils, and these dry, warm soils have pines and other associated species. Peatlands are a prominent feature and the bogs and fens with their wonderful assemblage of plants are found throughout the province. Marshes are essentially absent, but there are several small examples on the west coast of the island and the coast of Labrador.

Climate – Livyers try to compare one year with another but this is impossible because there is no "usual" weather. On the big picture, Labrador has a typical continental climate while Newfoundland's climate is hyperoceanic, affected by the ocean but influenced by the North American continent. All of the low pressure systems which originate in the Midwest or on the Eastern Seaboard end up in Newfoundland, complete with all the atmospheric pollutants. Newfoundland's climate does not lead to partitioning of the island: species which are considered continental and sub-continental in Europe (e.g., Leatherleaf, *Chamaedaphne calyculata*, and Lapland Rosebay, *Rhododendron lapponicum*) grow inland and on the coast in Newfoundland.

The province of Newfoundland and Labrador extends through more than 12 degrees of latitude. As a consequence, the growing season varies in its start and in its duration. On the Northern Peninsula, for example, the growing season is 150 days long at the base and 100 days at the tip of the peninsula. Blooming times have not been provided in the descriptions because they vary with location and can change from year to year.

Winters are unpredictable and changeable on the island, particularly on the eastern peninsulas. There may be a snow cover before heavy frost but often there is not. There will often be mild periods during the winter which lead to the freezing, thawing, and heaving of any plants which are not well rooted. Spring is not defined; in fact, there is no spring on the island. Wild fluctuations in temperature and precipitation cause considerable damage, and silver thaws break many branches. Labrador and the west coast of the island have better defined seasons.

Summer is fairly cool on the island, with warm days and cool nights; these conditions are enjoyable for tourists but cause problems for plant development. Plants must struggle to maintain growth in these conditions. Low temperatures and a constant wind cool leaf tissues and slow down life processes. The advantage of these conditions is that the roadsides are colourful, with bloom throughout the entire growing season. The most favourable growing conditions are found in central and southwestern Newfoundland and around Lake Melville in Labrador. These areas have sheltered valleys with warmer temperatures that do not cool as much at night because of their distance from the coast or their proximity to the mainland. Coastal regions, the Northern Peninsula, and northern Labrador are cooler, and the south coast is usually shrouded in fog for much of the summer. Autumn is often wet, although there are wonderful days to enjoy an afternoon of berry picking.

Elements in the Flora
In order to understand why the flora has an unusual mixture of species, the elements and the environmental factors which affect their distribution must be considered. The basic vegetation of the province is boreal forest and woods which look much like those of northern Ontario, northern Alberta, and southern Alaska. Labrador has tundra in its northern parts and plants of other floras extend into the island of Newfoundland and find their niches.

Plants with Southern Affinities – These species occur in Newfoundland but have their main range to the south and west of the island, and their continuous range on the mainland does not reach as far north as southern Labrador. This group includes the Coastal Plain Element, a group of species restricted, in Newfoundland, to bogs and sandy soils. They occur southwards along the Atlantic coast to the Pine Barrens of New Jersey. This group also includes temperate-boreal species which extend down the Alleghenian range. Their distribution is determined by temperature, soil, and a lack of certain plant associations (e.g., Eastern White Cedar). As these plants are adapted to regions which have higher summer temperatures and longer growing seasons than occur on the island, their distributions often show a clear northern boundary on the island and they are often restricted to warmer valleys. Plants from the south are triggered into growth by warmer temperatures and, on the continent, the temperature continues to get warmer in the spring. As Newfoundland's spring involves wild fluctuations in temperature with cold near the end of the season, these plants do not survive. Some, like the Mayflower (*Epigaea repens*), grow where the snow remains late into the season and they are protected from freezing and thawing. Many of the southern species grow along the coast where the winter temperatures are ameliorated. Some southern species are restricted to the nutrient-rich calcareous soils on the west coast. However, a lack of nutrients rarely eliminates a species entirely from the poorer sites of the east.

Plants with Arctic or Subarctic Affinities – Many of these only occur in a few alpine localities throughout the Maritimes, Gaspe, and New England but are found in Newfoundland and Labrador because of a combination of climatic and soil factors. Competition is also important for some arctic species. Although arctic plants can grow in a fairly broad range of temperatures, they cannot compete with the more vigorous boreal species, and so they grow in more marginal sites with less competition. They cannot tolerate high summer temperatures or shade. Many of these plants grow on the calcareous or serpentine sites of the west coast. These plants are found in Newfoundland's flora and most at higher elevations and along coastal cliffs. A few high arctic species extend south to the northern part of Labrador.

The Flora – The province is in the Boreal Forest Region of Canada. The central and western parts of the island and southern Labrador are forested, with treeless barrens restricted to higher elevations and latitudes. Most of the southern and eastern parts of the island and many parts of Labrador are covered by dwarf shrub heaths and bogs. The northern half of Labrador has tundra, with forest in sheltered valleys. The eastern parts of the island have several species in common with Europe. There are approximately 1,300 species of vascular plants in the province, 1,269 on the island and 674 in Labrador.

Prominent Families
Ericaceae (the Heath or Blueberry Family) has 37 species on the island and 23 in Labrador. They are all dwarf or small shrubs and found abundantly in all habitats. Many members give abundant harvests of berries each year (e.g., Partridgeberry/Redberry, *Vaccinium vitis-idaea*; and Blueberry, *Vaccinium angustifolium*).

Pinaceae (the Pine Family) is represented by eight species on the island and five in Labrador with White Spruce (*Picea glauca*), Balsam Fir (*Abies balsamea*), and Black Spruce (*Picea mariana*) dominating the vegetation.

Cyperaceae (the Sedge Family) has 139 species on the island and 83 in Labrador. Members are found mostly on peatlands and in other wet habitats.

Gramineae (the Grass Family) is found everywhere; it has 117 species on the island and 73 in Labrador.

Orchidaceae (the Orchid Family) has 45 species on the island and 10 in Labrador. Orchids are abundant, especially on peatlands.

Many other families like Compositae (the Daisy Family – 154 species in Newfoundland, 60 in Labrador), Betulaceae (the Birch Family – 13 species in Newfoundland, nine in Labrador), and others associate, one with the other, to form a mosaic of plant life in the province.

Peter J. Scott
2006

Acknowledgements

We would like to thank Dr. Alan Whittick for reviewing the text, and Iona Bulgin for editing the book. In addition, Sharon Wall, Peggy Ann Parsons, and Irene Ryan did us an enormous favour by transforming the original text into digital format.

Fragrant Waterlily

Nymphaea odorata Ait.
Waterlily Family
Nymphaeaceae

This exquisite plant rises from the murky depths of ponds. The emergence of the bud from the water and its opening likely suggested water nymphs to ancient Greeks; *Nymphaea* is the ancient name for water nymphs and *odorata* refers to the fragrance of the flowers.

The stem of the plant is a large branching rhizome that creeps across the mud or boggy bottom of a pond. A leaf develops from the rhizome and rises to the surface of the water. The length of the petiole is determined by the depth of the water when the leaf first forms. The leaves are nearly circular in outline, with a slit at the base to the point of attachment of the petiole; the upper surface is dark green, and the underside burgundy-coloured.

The fragrant flowers are the largest of any of the province's native plants. Many parts make up a blossom and may reveal something of the early history of some flowers. The four outermost parts, the sepals, are often purplish with rounded tips. There are then four outer and four inner white petals. The inner petals are more pointed. Within the petals eight series of many parts show a gradual transition from petals to stamens. This transition suggests that in some plants petals are modified stamens, as all the intermediates between petals and stamens are seen in this flower and some in other plants.

The fruit develops under water, and, when the seeds are ripe, it splits open. Each seed is enclosed in an air-filled sac, which serves as a float. When the seeds are released, they float to the surface in a group, separate, and float away. When the sac decays, the seeds sink to the bottom of the pond and grow, if the location is suitable.

The Fragrant Waterlily grows in the muddy ponds and bog pools of Newfoundland, except on the Northern Peninsula. It is often found growing with its near relatives, the Yellow Pondlilies (*Nuphar*), two of which are on the island. Yellow Pondlilies have yellow globose flowers and their leaves differ in shape and colour from the Fragrant Waterlily. The Fragrant Waterlily grows in most areas of North America.

Although this plant does not provide food for humans, moose eat the leaves, especially in late summer and early autumn, and caribou reportedly eat the leaves. Beavers eat the rhizomes and muskrats clean up any leftovers. Some Aboriginals, such as the Ojibwa, cooked the flower buds. Fry the buds in butter with chopped onions for five minutes.

Barachois Pond

2

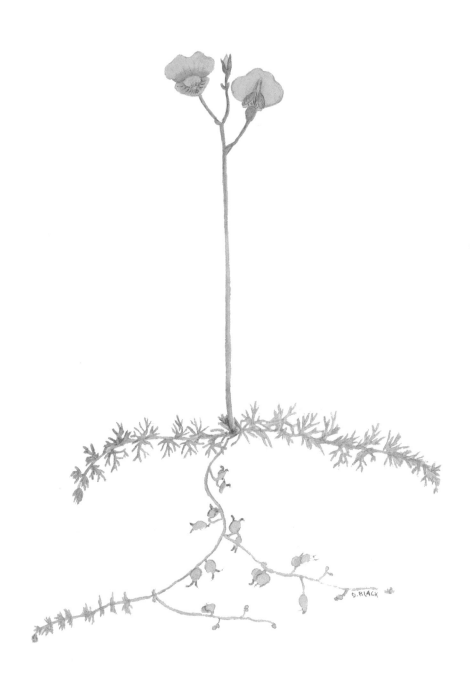

Flat-leafed Bladderwort

Utricularia intermedia Hayne
Bladderwort Family
Lentibulariaceae

Is the Flat-leafed Bladderwort a plant from science fiction? It would seem to be from another time, place, and situation, but it is alive and flourishing in Newfoundland and Labrador. It is one of several carnivorous plants in the province. *Utricularia* is from *utriculus*, a little bladder, and *intermedia* means intermediate.

This plant is unusual because it does not have any roots. It has a stem with leaves, bladders which are modified leaves, and flowers. The stem creeps over the mud in shallow water and bears many finely divided leaves that have flat divisions. The bladders are borne on separate branches and are about two millimetres long. Each bladder is shaped like a lima bean and has a trap door with four stiff bristles on the outside of the door. Water pumps empty the bladder so that there is reduced pressure inside. Special glands on the door secrete sugar in a mucilage which attracts tiny aquatic animals. If an animal touches one of the bristles, the door opens slightly, causing water and the victim to be drawn in. The door then closes and the animal is digested. These carnivorous plants carry on photosynthesis and, thus, manufacture their own food. They grow in a nutrient-poor environment and use insects and other small organisms as a source of nitrogen and other nutrients. The flowers are raised above the water's surface where they are visited by bees and other pollinators. They look like orchids from Central America.

The Flat-leafed Bladderwort grows in shallow ponds, pond edges, and bog holes all over Newfoundland and north to central Labrador (Goose Bay). This species occurs from Greenland to Alaska and south to Pennsylvania and California. There are four other species of *Utricularia* in Newfoundland.

Pacquet

5

Wild Calla

Calla palustris L.
Arum Family
Araceae

The Araceae is an example of a mainly tropical and subtropical family of plants that has a few representatives in temperate regions. The reverse also occurs: temperate region families with a few representatives in the tropics. The meaning of *Calla*, a name used by Roman natural historian Pliny the Elder (23-79 AD), is unknown. *Palustris* means of marshes.

Wild Calla looks similar to and is related to the Calla used in mortuary floral arrangements. It is a herbaceous plant with a long, stout, creeping rhizome and relatively large leaves. Shoots develop over two years. First- and second-year shoots are shown in the illustration. During the first year a shoot bears long-stalked, roundish leaves with a heart-shaped base (the smallest leaf in the illustration). In the second year, shoots produce a pair of leaves and an inflorescence consisting of the white spathe and finger-like spadix. The inflorescence is called a spadix and consists of many flowers crowded together in a finger-like structure. The lower flowers have both stamens and pistils but the upper flowers bear only stamens. The inflorescence is made conspicuous by the white spathe, which is a modified leaf. A nauseous odour emitted by the inflorescence attracts pollinators such as small flies, although snails also feed on the pollen. The fruit are red berries and each contains a few seeds.

This species is found in a few localities on the west coast, in central Newfoundland, and north to central Labrador. It grows along the edges of ponds and in bog pools. It is also found west to Alaska and south to Pennsylvania. In Eurasia, it is found in central and northern Europe and east to Siberia.

In Lapland several centuries ago, the rhizomes of Wild Calla were ground and used in bread, but because of the plant's rarity in Newfoundland and Labrador this practice should not be encouraged.

Beothuk Park

Buckbean

Menyanthes trifoliata L.
Gentian Family
Gentianaceae

This is a stiff and formal-looking plant with neat crisp leaves and a spire of fringed white flowers. *Menyanthes*, a name used by Theophrastus (370-285 BC, Greek, known as the Father of Botany), means disclosing a flower and refers to the way that the flower progressively expands. *Trifoliata* means three-leafed.

Buckbean is a perennial herb of boreal regions. It has a thick creeping rhizome sheathed by the bases of the long petioles. The three leaflets are somewhat fleshy and smooth. The leafless flower stalk rises from the rhizome and bears flowers that open from the base of the stalk upwards. These flowers turn brown rapidly after they have been picked.

The flowers are fascinating, as are the flowers of many aquatic plants. The five-lobed calyx is short and tubular and the corolla has a short, funnel-shaped base and five long lobes. Each lobe is bearded with a dense covering of coarse white hairs, and the stamens are attached to the funnel portion of the corolla. The hairs prevent small insects, which could not effect pollination, from crawling to the base of the flower and stealing nectar. The style is stout and persistent on top of the seed capsule. In some flowers, such as the one illustrated, the style is longer than the stamens, while in others the reverse occurs. The capsule is thin-walled and breaks open irregularly. This means that the seeds are released over a longer period of time and will have a better chance of becoming dispersed.

This species grows in shallow water and pond margins all across Newfoundland, north to northern Labrador, and west to Alaska. It occurs south to West Virginia and Nebraska and also in Eurasia. This is an easy species to identify. Some botanists include the Buckbean in the Gentian Family, but others prefer to give it its own family.

Tilt Cove

Silverweed

Potentilla anserina L.
Rose Family
Rosaceae

It is a surprise to find this bit of sunshine among the sedges, rushes, and grasses that grow along the water's edge. *Potentilla*, meaning powerful, was the name originally used for this plant which was once thought to have strong medicinal powers. *Anserina* means of geese.

Silverweed has some similarities to its relative, the strawberry: its rosette of leaves, stolons, and flower, except for colour, are similar, and its fruit looks like a dry strawberry. Much of Silverweed is covered with fine white hairs, especially the lower surface of the leaves which is densely clothed with shiny hairs. The calyx and corolla have their parts in fives, but a close examination of the calyx in the illustration shows 10 sepals. The smaller segments are known as the calyculus. Each of the five sepals has a small stipule at its base on each side and the two stipules of adjacent sepals are fused along their margins to form the narrow segments.

This species grows along the shores of ponds and by the ocean throughout Newfoundland and north to central Labrador. It is also found in Eurasia and across much of North America. Egede's Silverweed (*Potentilla egedii* Wormsk), similar to this species except that it lacks the abundant hairs, also occurs in this province.

Silverweed was used as an astringent in medicine for diarrhea. This plant has also been used as food. In the early spring, the raw or cooked root is said to taste like parsnips. The root is also used as a source of red dye for wool and other fabrics.

Bellevue Beach

10

Sea Rocket

Cakile edentula (Bigel.) Hook.
Mustard Family
Cruciferae

Poke around in the mats of Sea Rocket on the beach and find a fruit; it looks like an ice cream cone. *Cakile* is an archaic Arabic name and *edentula* means without teeth.

These succulent annuals branch and spread on the beach and form a patch about 50 centimetres in diameter. The leaves are broader towards the tip and have wavy toothing along the margins. The petals vary from pale pink or purple to white.

The fruit, a silique, is divided transversely, producing two one-seeded parts. The fruit is corky when it is mature and dry. The lower portion of the fruit remains on the plant; it has one seed or is sometimes seedless. The upper portion has one seed and it separates and floats away to a distant beach.

Sea Rocket grows on beaches and the seashore. It is found in coastal Newfoundland and north to Labrador (Forteau), south to South Carolina, the Great Lakes region, from southern Alaska to California, Iceland, Azores, Norway, and northern Russia.

Fishers in Labrador used to collect this plant for greens. The young foliage and fruit can be added to salads.

Bay d'Espoir

13

Sea Lungwort

Mertensia maritima (L.) S.F. Gray
Borage Family
Boraginaceae

The Sea Lungwort produces smaller flowers than those of its close relative, the Virginia Bluebell. The name *Mertensia* commemorates Franz Karl Mertens (1764-1831), a German botanist, and *maritima* means of seashores.

This plant spreads over the rocks on many of the province's beaches and often forms quite large patches by the end of the summer. Its leaves are covered with small flakes of wax exuded by the leaf; this is what gives the plant its whitened appearance and makes the leaves blend in with the rocks. The clusters of small bell-like flowers at the end of the branches show an interesting colour change also seen in other plants of this family. The flowers are rose-pink when they open, but turn blue with age. This colour contrast for attracting insect pollinators is also characteristic of Forget-me-nots (*Myosotis* spp.) and Soldiers-and-Sailors (*Pulmonaria officinalis* L.).

Sea Lungwort, also called Oyster Plant, is a good example of a strand plant. These beach plants have seeds that float in salt water to new areas. Sea Lungwort is found on the rocky beaches of northern Europe and Greenland. In North America it is found on the shores of the Arctic Ocean and the Bering Sea, and extends as far south as Vancouver on the west coast and Massachusetts on the east. It is restricted to seaside beaches and is dispersed by the sea. Salt water damages plants by dehydrating plant tissue, but Sea Lungwort seeds are well equipped for sea travel as their hard, waxy coat and corky layer make them buoyant. The buoyant seeds float to a distant bay and become established on the beach.

This plant grows on beaches throughout Newfoundland and north to southern Labrador, but particularly in sheltered areas. It is the only member of the genus in this province and the only plant on beaches with pink or blue bell-shaped flowers.

Green Point Campground,
Gros Morne National Park

Beach Pea

Lathyrus japonicus Willd.
Pea Family
Leguminosae

Beach Pea is such a delight; it forms a fresh-looking green circle on beaches and has rich burgundy flowers. *Lathyrus*, a legume named by Theophrastus, is said to be derived from *la* (very) and *thuros* (passionate); the original plant was used as an aphrodisiac. *Japonicus* means Japanese. This species is also known as *Lathyrus maritimus*.

The plant is somewhat fleshy and its strong root system is an adaptation to an unstable substrate. Lumps along the roots are root nodules which harbour bacteria that transform atmospheric nitrogen into a chemical form that plants can use. This process, called nitrogen fixation, is common in leguminous plants. The compound leaves of this plant have four to 10 leaflets and the inflorescence has three to 10 flowers.

This species is found around the seashores and beaches of inland waters of the northern hemisphere, including coastal Newfoundland, and north to northern Labrador. A similar species, the Vetchling (*Lathyrus palustris* L.), has small, one-lobed stipules, little flaps found where the leaf attaches to the stem, while the Beach Pea has larger, two-lobed stipules.

Young pods can be eaten, and young shoots and seeds have been consumed as famine food. However, the plant contains chemicals (alkaloids) which can cause liver damage.

Hare Bay

Sea Lavender

Limonium carolinianum (Walt.) Britt.
Leadwort Family
Plumbaginaceae

The flowers of Sea Lavender look like those of statice, to which it is related; both are used in dried flower arrangements. *Limonium* is from the ancient Greek name, *Leimonion*, which means a marsh; *Carolinianum* means of Carolina.

The leaves of Sea Lavender are thick and shiny. There are several leaves at the base of the leafless inflorescence. Flowers are in two forms; one has styles longer than the other, an adaptation to promote cross-pollination. The corolla is lavender in colour and fits in the smooth and hairless tubular calyx. The calyx remains on the plant and the seed capsule develops in it.

This species grows in salt marshes and pools along the edges of sheltered beaches and lagoons of western and northeastern Newfoundland and north to southern Labrador. It is also found along the coasts of eastern Quebec, the Maritime provinces, and south to Florida and Texas.

Hare Bay

Arnica Ragwort

Senecio pseudo-arnica Less.
Daisy Family
Compositae

It is a surprise to clamber down a cliff and find such a large, exotic-looking flower by the seashore. *Senecio*, from the Latin *senex*, an old man, refers to the hoary nature of many of the species. *Pseudo-arnica* means false *Arnica*.

This stout plant has a substantial root system typical of plants growing on unstable beaches. Much of the plant has a cobwebby coating of hairs. The lower leaves often wither early in the season and the upper leaves are waxy and slightly succulent. The large flower heads make the species appear exotic, and the fruit have many hairs to carry them aloft.

Arnica Ragwort is a halophyte. It grows in salty soil and sand around the coast of this province, from central Labrador to Maine. It also occurs from Vancouver, north through the Aleutians, and into northeastern Asia.

Cape Norman

Blue Flag

Iris versicolor L.
Iris Family
Iridaceae

One highlight of late spring is seeing a wet area adorned with Blue Flag flowers under a sunny sky. *Iris* means the rainbow and *versicolor* means variously coloured.

Blue Flag has a stout rhizome that may be buried or near the surface of the soil. The leaves arise from the rhizome up to 50 centimetres in a fan-like arrangement. They are folded along their length and arranged in two opposite ranks, so that the inner leaves are sheathed by each successive leaf.

The flowers of irises have their parts modified. There are six mainly blue petals; the three largest that droop are called falls, and the three smaller erect ones standards. In the cultivated German Bearded Iris, the standards are large. Each of the three styles of Blue Flag, which curve over the falls, is large, flattened, and petal-like, and beneath each is a stamen.

The Blue Flag grows in marshes, meadows, and along rivers and ponds all over the island and north to central Labrador. Another species, the Beach-head Flag (*Iris setosa* Pall.), grows on sea cliffs, beaches, and other places near the sea around the coast. It is generally smaller than Blue Flag, with bluish-green leaves and one-to-two-centimetre-long standards, compared with the Blue Flag with its green leaves and over-two-centimetre-long standards. The Blue Flag occurs from Newfoundland to Manitoba and south to Virginia.

This plant should not be eaten. The rhizome contains irisin, an emetic and cathartic, which, if ingested can cause severe illness and often death. In some parts of Newfoundland Blue Flag is known as chirpers because children split a section of leaf and use it to make chirping sounds.

Baie Verte

Flexuous Bittercress

Cardamine flexuosa With.
Mustard Family
Cruciferae

The delicate leaves of Flexuous Bittercress contrast with those of the grasses and sedges amongst which it grows. *Cardamine* is from the Greek *kardamon*, which was the name given by Dioscorides, a first-century Greek physician, to a type of cress. *Flexuosa* means flexuous.

This biennial species, like many members of this family of plants, forms a rosette during the first year, and flowers and seeds in the second. The stem, which is hairy at the base but otherwise hairless, is erect when the plant is growing on land, but trails when growing wholly or partially submersed. The small Jacob's-Ladder-like leaves are dainty in appearance. The terminal leaflet is always broader than the others. The flowers, which have four petals and six stamens, are not showy. The fruit is long and slender and of the type known as silique. Siliques have three parts: a frame with a membrane stretched over it, seeds attached along the frame on both sides of the membrane, and two covers that attach all around to the frame. The dispersal of seeds from siliques is violent. The covers become detached at the base first. As they roll up rapidly towards the tip, the seeds are torn off and flung outwards. Rain or nearby water disperse the seeds farther.

Flexuous Bittercress grows in wet and moist habitats in western and eastern Newfoundland. This species was introduced from Europe to a few locations on the island and in Quebec. There are three other species on the island.

This species is reputed to be a good substitute for the favourite salad green, Watercress. Carefully wash any plants collected from water.

La Scie

Canadian Burnet

Sanguisorba canadensis L.
Rose Family
Rosaceae

The Canadian Burnet rises stiffly on many parts of Newfoundland and Labrador. *Sanguisorba* means to absorb blood and comes from its use in folk medicine. *Canadensis* means Canadian.

This plant's distinctive leaves resemble Dogberry leaves arising from the bog or wet ground where this species grows. The flowering stems arise from amongst the basal leaves. Before the buds open, the spike looks like a beaded caterpillar. The bottle-brush effect comes with the opening of the flowers which have no petals although it looks as if there are four tiny whitish-green ones. These structures are in fact petal-like sepals. The four stamens of each flower are prominent as the filaments are flattened, enlarged, and white in colour. These filaments attract insect pollinators, for whom nectar is provided at the bases of the stamens. The flowers partly close to protect the nectar from being washed away in rainy weather.

Canadian Burnet grows in bogs and wet areas all over the island and north to northern Labrador. It occurs west to Manitoba, and south into New England, and down through the mountains to Georgia.

It has been suggested that the young leaves of Canadian Burnet be used, as the European species have, for salads.

Baie Verte

Joe-Pye-Weed

Eupatorium maculatum L.
Daisy Family
Compositate

This plant's growth into a neat clump gives it a manicured appearance. *Eupatorium* commemorates Mithridates Eupator (132-63 BC), who used a related species in medicine. *Maculatum* means mottled.

Joe-Pye-Weed can grow to over one metre in height. The stem, which has coarse leaves borne in whorls of four or five, is mottled or sometimes evenly suffused with purple. As the leaves vary considerably in shape, colour, and number in a whorl, it is difficult to imagine that these different plants belong to the same species. The rosy-coloured composite flowers are insignificant individually, but in a cluster they attract pollinating insects. This clumping of florets in composite flowers and grouping of composite flowers makes a lot of a little.

This species grows in moist areas – meadows, riverbanks, and shores of ponds throughout the island of Newfoundland. It also occurs across Canada and south to North Carolina in the east and New Mexico in the west. There is only one species of Joe-Pye-Weed in Newfoundland, and, since it is so distinctive, it should not cause any confusion.

Conne Pond, Bay d'Espoir

Turtlehead

Chelone glabra L.
Figwort Family
Scrophulariaceae

As people and animals are generally more fascinating than plants, it is not uncommon for animal forms to be imagined in flowers, roots, stems, and leaves. This is the case with Turtlehead. *Chelone* is Greek for turtle and indicates that the flower resembles the head of a turtle. *Glabra* means smooth.

Turtlehead, like Joe-Pye-Weed, grows in wet habitats which often feature a variety of untidy-looking plants. These two stand out because of their dark green leaves and tidy mound shapes. Turtlehead has opposite dark green leaves that vary from oval- to lance-shaped. The inflorescence has many overlapping parts. Each flower bud has a rounded scale-like leaf that covers it before it starts to expand. The five sepals are separate and overlapping. This is unusual for a flower that has a corolla consisting of fused petals as the flowers generally also have the sepals fused into a tube. The corolla is creamy white, with a white beard on the lower lip. There are usually five stamens in this family, but in Turtlehead one is sterile and remains a short green filament. It is called a staminode.

This plant grows in wet, sheltered habitats across the island except the Northern Peninsula. It is a variable species, occurring throughout much of eastern North America. This is the only species found in Newfoundland.

Conne Pond, Bay d'Espoir

Marsh Marigold

Caltha palustris L.
Buttercup Family
Ranunculaceae

The name Marigold has been given to several yellow-flowered plants. Originally Mary's Gold, it was a name given in dedication to the Virgin Mary. *Caltha* is from *calathos*, which means cup, and *palustris* means of swamps.

This plant has roots adapted to a wet environment. The root tips of plants generally bear small root hairs that increase the surface area of the root and the potential uptake of water and dissolved nutrients. *Caltha* and other marsh plants lack these superfluous hairs. A hollow stem and large leaves reflect the watery environment of the Marsh Marigold.

The flowers have five bright yellow sepals, and the petals are reduced to nectaries. If the flowers are not visited by beetles or other insects, then pollination can be effected by rain. A large drop collects in the flower and pollen floats to the stigmas. The seeds utilize water for dispersal, as they have fleshy attachments that provide buoyancy.

Marsh Marigolds grow in swamps, wet meadows, and wet woods of western Newfoundland, in a few localities in the eastern part of the island, and north to southern Labrador. They are found west to Alaska and south to Tennessee and Nebraska, and are also widely distributed in Eurasia.

The young leaves of Marsh Marigold are edible, but only after being boiled for about an hour with several changes of water. This plant contains anemonin, a harmful substance causing gastric upset and mouth sores, which is destroyed by boiling or drying the plant.

Corner Brook

Northern Willowherb

Epilobium glandulosum Lehm.
Evening Primrose Family
Onagraceae

A name is often bestowed on one plant that suggests its resemblance to another. These small *Epilobium* species are herbs that have willow-shaped leaves. *Epilobium*, from the Greek *epi* meaning upon and *lobon* meaning capsule, refers to the fact that they have inferior ovaries, ovaries with the sepals, petals, and stamens attached to the top. *Glandulosum* means bearing glands.

The stems may exceed 50 centimetres in height and may be unbranched or branched. The stem is somewhat square in cross-section and hairless at the bottom but minutely hairy towards the top, often with small glands. The glands look like small lumps and secrete a sticky substance. The flowers are small with four sepals, petals, and stamens, and the capsule wall splits along four lines. The fifth part of the capsule in the illustration is the central core (placenta) to which the seeds are attached.

The seeds are well adapted to float on the wind for a considerable distance. A tuft of flying hairs on the end of the seed acts as a parachute. To allow for day-to-day variation in wind intensity, the capsule splits open gradually and sheds seeds over a period of a week or more.

Northern Willowherb grows in cooler climates. It is common all over Newfoundland in wet or boggy soil, and north to central Labrador. It occurs west to Alaska, south to Vermont in the east, and Colorado in the west. It also grows in eastern Asia. In Newfoundland and Labrador, there are 12 species of willowherb-type *Epilobium* and two larger ones, Fireweed and River Beauty. The willowherbs are variable and difficult to distinguish. There are some white-flowered species, but of the pink-flowered willowherbs this species is the most common.

Baie Verte

Small Purple Fringed Orchid

Platanthera psycodes (L.) Lindl.
Orchid Family
Orchidaceae

Although orchids are considered exotic and beautiful, they are beautiful but not really exotic. Of the 43 species in Newfoundland and 15 in Labrador, this is one of the prettiest. *Platanthera* means broad anther. *Psycodes* is from Psyche, the lover of Cupid. In mythology Psyche was usually represented as a fairy with wings because she was considered the personification of the human soul, and in very ancient times the soul was thought of as a bird or an insect.

This orchid can range in height from about 30 centimetres to almost one metre. The strap-like leaves are found along the stem. The fragrant flowers, which vary in colour from deep pink to white, are borne in large spikes. The lip has three segments, and insects land on it to sip the nectar and simultaneously pollinate the flower. The thickened stalk behind the flower is the ovary, and, because it is found below the petals, it is called an inferior ovary. When a flower first begins to form, it has the lip uppermost. During development the ovary twists through 180 degrees so that when the flower opens, the lip is hanging down. This twisting is seen in an old seed capsule, or by examining the ovary itself. The inversion of the flower during development is called resupination and is found in the Orchid Family and a few other plant families.

The Small Purple Fringed Orchid is found in wet meadows and bogs all over the island but infrequently on the Northern Peninsula. It grows west to Ontario and south to Tennessee.

Orchids are lovely but ecologically fragile plants. The flowers should be admired, smelled, and enjoyed, but left growing.

Lomond

Spotted Touch-me-not

Impatiens capensis Meerb.
Touch-me-not Family
Balsaminaceae

Spotted Touch-me-not, or Jewelweed, are appropriate names for this plant. This gem of a plant contrasts startlingly with its habitat. *Impatiens* is Latin for impatient and refers to the sudden bursting of the capsules when they are touched. *Capensis* means of the Cape, because it was originally thought that this plant was introduced into Europe from the Cape of Good Hope.

This plant reflects its wet habitat: it looks and feels watery or dewy; the stem is almost transparent; and the leaves are frail, thin, and fleshy. Along the petioles of the leaves are short stalks, which usually have small crystals of sugar on their ends. These nectaries, with the exuded nectar crystallized on their tips, are called extra-floral nectaries. Their function is not fully understood but it has been suggested that they attract ants, which protect the plant from aphids and other insect pests. The flower has a complex structure with brightly coloured petals and sepals. The colour and the amount of spotting vary. The large pouch protruding behind the flower is a sepal with a slender recurved nectar spur. The anthers are fused around the stigma and ovary.

The seed capsule, which gives this plant its common name, is an example of an explosive fruit. The outer wall consists of five sections which are swollen at their upper ends where the seeds are located. Tension in the wall is created by a layer of large water-engorged cells that line the inner surface. When the fruit is mature, the slightest disturbance causes the outer wall to break apart and the sections to roll up inwards. The seeds are thrown in all directions for a few metres, and, should they fall into the water, they float for some distance. It takes considerable patience or a magician's hand to capture the seeds of this beauty.

The Spotted Touch-me-not grows by pools and streams or in moist woods across the island portion of the province. It also occurs west to Alaska and south to Florida and Oklahoma. The Pale Touch-me-not (*Impatiens pallida* Nutt.) also grows in Newfoundland. It is pale yellow with red spots and its nectar spur is only one-fifth to one-fourth as long as the pouch, compared with one-third to one-half as long in this species.

Although this plant looks tender and juicy, it is reputed to be poisonous and so should be avoided.

Doyles, Codroy Valley

Purple Loosestrife

Lythrum salicaria L.
Loosestrife Family
Lythraceae

The flower spires of Purple Loosestrife add a formal aspect to an otherwise informal assemblage of swamp plants. *Lythrum* is the name Dioscorides gave to this species. *Salicaria* means like a willow and refers to the shape of the leaves.

This hairy plant can grow to over one metre in height. The leaves are arranged along the stem in pairs or in threes. The flowers of Purple Loosestrife exhibit interesting structural variations first described by Charles Darwin. Three different forms of these flowers are found on different plants and represent a complex pollination mechanism. The flowers have six petals and differ in the length of their stamens and styles, which can be long, medium, or short. All of the flowers have 12 stamens in two sets of six and a single style. Long-styled flowers have six short and six medium stamens with the style projecting beyond them; medium-styled flowers, six short and six long stamens with a medium-length style; and short-styled flowers, six medium and six long stamens with a short style. The long styles are three times as long as the short styles, and the stigmas and anthers differ in size from one form of flower to another. The short and medium anthers have yellow pollen which has fat as a stored food, and the long stamens have green pollen which has starch as a stored food. The long-styled flowers produce the largest seeds and the short-styled the smallest. All three types are equally common in any area. Long styles must be pollinated by pollen from long stamens to produce seeds, and the same applies to the other lengths. In addition to this fastidiousness, it has been found that usually only a single species of bee visits Purple Loosestrife and that this bee rarely visits the flowers of any other species.

Purple Loosestrife was introduced to Newfoundland from Europe and is usually found near seaports such as St. John's and Corner Brook. It generally grows in wet areas by ponds or in roadside ditches. This is the only species in the province. It might initially be confused with members of the Mint Family (Labiatae), but not after comparing the six petals of Loosestrife with the hooded flowers of the mints. This species also grows west to Quebec and Minnesota and south to West Virginia. In many localities, it is an aggressive invader and has caused environmental problems.

Flatwater Pond

Tall Meadowrue

Thalictrum pubescens Pursh
Buttercup Family
Ranunculaceae

The Tall Meadowrue, a graceful plant of moist habitats, has leaves like large fronds of Maidenhair Fern. *Thalictrum* was a plant name used by Dioscorides and *pubescens* means hairy.

Flowering stalks, which rise up to two metres from the rosettes of basal leaves, have clustered flower buds on the tips of the branches reminiscent of broccoli. The flowers of *Thalictrum*, which are grouped in open clusters, are dioecious, producing male and female flowers on separate plants. However, some female flowers may have a few stamens (male parts); this is termed polygamy and is shown in the lower right of the illustration. The female flowers are inconspicuous, but the male flowers catch the eye because the stamen filaments are white and club-shaped, a shape adapted for wind-pollination. Since the filament is broad, it will be moved by breezes; this aids in shedding pollen, which can be blown to female flowers on nearby plants. The fruit are found in clusters late in the summer, and, with ribs along their length, they look like anise seeds.

The Tall Meadowrue is found throughout the island and north to south-central Labrador in wet meadows, along streams, and in other moist areas. This species grows west to Ontario and south to Georgia. There is also a tiny species (Alpine Meadowrue, *Thalictrum alpinum* L.) on hilltops in western parts of the island.

Baie Verte

Wild Mint

Mentha arvensis L.
Mint Family
Labiatae

Mint is named for Mentha, a naiad, who was the mistress of Pluto, the ruler of Hades. Proserpine, Pluto's jealous wife, trampled Mentha underfoot and transformed her into a lowly plant, doomed to be trodden upon forever. Pluto softened Mentha's fate by willing that the more mint plants are trodden upon, the sweeter will be the scent that arises. *Arvensis* means of cultivated ground.

The stems of Wild Mint, which are square in cross-section and bear opposite leaves, arise from a somewhat fleshy underground rhizome. There is considerable variation in the degree of hairiness of these plants. The Wild Mint in this province tends to have hairs on the stems and leaves. The scent of mint is an aromatic oil produced by glandular scales on the surface of the stem and leaves. If the plant is crushed, oil is released and vaporizes. The scent is lost when the plant is dried and stored for a long time, as the oil evaporates.

The flowers differ from those of other members of the Mint Family in that the corolla is star-shaped, not two-lipped.

Wild Mint is found along streams and ponds and in damp soil across the island and north to central Labrador (Goose Bay). It is circumboreal in distribution and occurs in most parts of North America. It is the only native species of *Mentha*. The upper leaves of Heart Mint (*Mentha cardiaca* Baker), introduced into Newfoundland, are small and reduced compared to its lower leaves. In Wild Mint the upper leaves are smaller but similar in appearance to the lower leaves.

Mint sauce or jelly is commonly used with meats like lamb and veal. Fresh mint is used to make mint juleps, dried to make mint tea, chopped and added to a salad, or dropped into a pot of fresh peas. Mint tea is effective for relieving gas although they may cause heartburn.

Baie Verte

Creeping Buttercup

Ranunculus repens L.
Buttercup Family
Ranunculaceae

In spite of the problem of eradicating Creeping Buttercup if it becomes established in a garden, it can brighten an otherwise repulsive dank ditch. *Ranunculus*, Latin for little frog, was used by Pliny, because these plants grow in frog habitats. *Repens* means creeping.

This perennial species has thick whitish roots and long trailing branches produced from the basal leaves, which root and produce new plants. This characteristic gives it its specific name. The basal leaves are divided into three distinct leaflets which, in turn, are deeply lobed. The dark green leaves are often mottled with white, as shown in the illustration.

The deep yellow flowers are unique amongst flowering plants in that the yellow pigment is dissolved in oil contained within a layer of cells in the petals. Pigment is usually present as crystals which refract light. Just below these pigment-filled cells in the Creeping Buttercup is a layer of cells packed with starch; this acts like the silvering on the back of a mirror, giving the glossy petals for determining whether a person likes butter. An attractive double-flowered form grows in certain localities on the island; this could make a lovely garden plant if it were watched for spreading. The flower is followed by a cluster of dry flattened fruit with short curved beaks.

Creeping Buttercups are found in wet open areas, ditches, and gardens throughout Newfoundland and north to central Labrador (Cartwright). A rapidly spreading weed naturalized from Europe, this species occurs west to Ontario and south to North Carolina as well as on the west coast of North America. The Common Buttercup (*Ranunculus acris* L.), the other common species on the island, grows upright, has no runners, and has basal leaves which are deeply lobed but not divided into leaflets.

These two common buttercups are inedible as they contain the irritant protoanemoin. If animals eat buttercups, they suffer from severe irritation of the mouth and digestive tract; they may also become blind, and, in severe cases of poisoning, death follows convulsions. It is said that beggars in the Middle Ages would scratch their limbs and rub in buttercup juice to produce running sores as an aid to procuring alms.

Baie Verte

Blue Marsh Violet

Viola cucullata Ait.
Violet Family
Violaceae

Violets have been celebrated in prose and verse since early times, usually in association with forest creatures. The meaning of *Viola*, the ancient name for violets, has been lost in time. *Cucullata* means hooded and refers to the young leaves, which are rolled inwards.

The broad heart-shaped leaves of the Blue Marsh Violet vary considerably in shape. The bases of the petioles and the stipules cover the short stout stem and are used to identify this species. The dainty flowers, which arise singly from the stem, have five petals – two upper and three lower. The central lower petal is prolonged backwards to form a nectar-bearing spur, while the two lateral petals have a beard of club-shaped hairs.

The pigment which gives the flower its blue colour has been used to determine the acidity or alkalinity (pH) of chemical solutions. The pigment can be extracted by barely covering flowers with boiling water and letting it stand for 24 hours. After straining, the infusion can be tested. It will be blue, but the addition of acid such as lemon juice turns the solution purple or reddish. It will turn green and later yellow by adding an alkaline substance such as baking soda. When the solutions are standardized and a colour chart produced, violet blossom infusion can be used to determine pH, a practice that was common in Europe during the Middle Ages.

This species is found throughout the island Newfoundland and also occurs west to northern Ontario and south to Tennessee. There are 12 species of violets in Newfoundland, of which five have blue flowers. The Marsh Violet, as its name suggests, grows in damp places such as the edges of streams, wet meadows, and bogs.

Violet leaves and flowers can be eaten. The leaves, which are rich in vitamins A and C, are used in salads and as steamed greens. The flowers can be used to make jelly and syrup or candied to decorate baked goods.

Baie Verte

Northern White Violet

Viola pallens (Banks) Brainerd
Violet Family
Violaceae

Almost anything in miniature has more charm than a full-scale version. The detail and dainty structure of a miniature is fascinating, and such is the case with this little flower. *Viola* is the classical name for violets and *pallens* means pale.

This plant rises from slender rhizomes and is only about eight centimetres tall at maturity. The nectar collects in a spur which projects behind the flower. The spur is an outpocketing of the lowest petal. The purple nectar guides on the lowest three petals direct an insect's attention to the centre of the flower where it can insert its tongue and sip nectar, pollinating the flower in the process.

Only two or three genera of plants in the world have a style like that of *Viola*. Most styles are solid with a sticky stigma on the tip; the pollen adheres to the stigma and a pollen tube grows down through the style. In *Viola*, however, the style is hollow and has no stigma. The pipe-like structure has a sharp elbow bend just above the ovary, and a right-angle bend at its tip. There is a small opening at the tip. The interior of the style is filled with a mucous secretion. When pressed by an insect, the style bends at the elbow and this pressure forces some mucous to protrude from the tip. Pollen adheres to this substance, and, after the insect releases the pressure from the style, the mucous is withdrawn into the style, where the pollen can germinate.

The Northern White Violet blooms early in the spring on bogs and other wet habitats throughout Newfoundland and north to northern Labrador. It occurs west to Alaska and south to the hills of Alabama. There are 12 species of violets in Newfoundland and six species in Labrador, of which four are white with purple veining.

The small leaves, rich in vitamins A and C, are used in spring salads. Candied violet flowers make a special treat.

Baie Verte

Pitcher Plant

Sarracenia purpurea L.
Pitcher Plant Family
Sarraceniaceae

Another common name for Newfoundland and Labrador's provincial flower is Huntsman's Cup, as hunters would slake their thirst with water in the leaves. *Sarracenia* commemorates Dr. Michel Sarrasin de l'Etang, an early-eighteenth-century physician in Quebec, who first sent specimens of this plant to Europe; and *purpurea* means purple.

The leaves of this plant are remarkable. They arise in a rosette and are bright purplish-green with dark red veining. It is thought that the pitcher leaf evolved by the rolling of the blade and then fusion of the two free edges to give a flap along its length. The leaf is designed to trap insects, which serve as a supplemental source of nitrogen. This allows the species to grow in habitats such as bogs where nitrogen is not readily available. Flies and other small insects are attracted to the pitcher by nectar secreted in the throat of the leaf. In an attempt to reach the nectar, they creep down the lip of the leaf. Its waxy surface makes the lip slippery. When the insect attempts to get out, the surface and downward-pointing stiff hairs prevent it from doing so and it falls into water that collects in the pitcher. Bacteria digest the insect and release nutrients for the plant's use. Several small animals and insect larvae have adapted to living in the pitchers.

The flowers have five stiff persistent sepals and five purple-red petals which fall off a few days after the flower opens. The style is expanded above the ovary into an umbrella-like structure which has small stigmatic surfaces at the tips of the five lobes and which spreads over the stamens.

The Pitcher Plant grows on bogs all over the island and north to central Labrador. It also occurs west to the Yukon and south to Florida and Louisiana.

La Scie

Bog Aster

Aster nemoralis Ait.
Daisy Family
Compositae

Nemoralis means of woodland, and, since Bog Asters grow on bogs and in other wet habitats, one wonders what happened when this species was first described and named. *Aster* means star and refers to its starry flowers.

Bog Aster's long slender rhizomes creep just under the surface of sphagnum moss and form a network from which the stems arise. This species of *Aster* is particularly dainty and neat in appearance. The unbranched stems are generally about 10 centimetres in height but they can grow to about 50 centimetres. The numerous leaves have untoothed margins. A careful examination of the margins reveals that they are neatly rolled under and have tiny stiff hairs. Each plant typically terminates in a single flower, but it is not unusual to find plants with two or, rarely, three flowers. The leaves rapidly diminish in size upward until, below the flowers, they are just tiny scale-like bracts. The ray florets are a clear lilac-purple, but one rare form has white flowers. The seeds have a tuft of fine hairs that acts like a parachute to carry it on the wind.

The Bog Aster grows on bogs and other wet habitats across the island, although there have been no reports of it from the northern part of the Northern Peninsula. It also occurs in central Labrador (Goose Bay). There are 13 other species of *Aster* but the one found on the bog and looking like the illustration is this distinctive species.

Bay d'Espoir

Goldthread

Coptis groenlandica (Oeder) Fern.
Buttercup Family
Ranunculaceae

Many years ago a pharmaceutical firm wrote to a missionary in Labrador and offered 50 cents a pound for dried Goldthread roots to be used for dyeing. The offer was ignored and so the habitat remains undisturbed. *Coptis* is from the Greek *coptein* meaning to cut and refers to the divided leaves. *Groenlandica* means of Greenland. This species is also known as *Coptis trifolia*.

The thread-like underground rhizome of this plant is often golden yellow, giving rise to its common name. The shiny, evergreen leaves are leathery in texture and usually arise singly or in twos or threes from the bog; when no flower is present, the whole plant is easily overlooked. The three leaflets are basically three-lobed and have sharp pointed teeth along their margins. The flowers are borne singly on thread-like stalks which appear briefly early in the spring. The petal-like sepals vary in number from five to seven. The petals are entirely absent. The ovaries, which are separate from each other, vary in number from three to seven. They have long-curved stigmas, and, when mature are long, narrow, many-seeded, and borne aloft on little stalks.

This dainty plant grows on bogs and in damp mossy woods across Newfoundland and Labrador. It also grows from Greenland to Manitoba and south to Tennessee. It flowers for a short period and the green fruit are not visible without a search. Goldthread is usually identified by its distinctive leaves.

Baie Verte

Grass Pink

Calopogon tuberosus (L.) BSP
Orchid Family
Orchidaceae

This is one of three short, pink bog orchids. The flowers are upside down but there is a good reason for this. *Calopogon* is from the Greek *calos* (beautiful) and *pogon* (beard). *Tuberosus* means tuberous.

The flowering stem, which has one or two leaves, arises from an ovoid corm below the bog's surface. Plants in this province usually have one or two flowers, but farther south the plants have up to 20 or 30 flowers. The lip is at the top of the flower rather than below, and the knobby hairs resemble stamens. Visiting bees must be a specific size to activate the hinge in the lip: small bees are too light and large bees are too heavy. However, medium-sized bees are heavy enough to cause the lip to lower; they would usually have already visited a flower, and are therefore dusted with pollen. A bee first rubs against a flower's stigma, where it deposits pollen; it then touches the anthers and picks up more pollen before flying off to another flower. When the bee moves on, the lip springs back up, ready for the next visitor.

Grass Pink grows on bogs across the island, north to central Labrador (Goose Bay), and throughout eastern Canada and the United States.

Tilting, Fogo Island

Rose Pogonia

Pogonia ophioglossoides (L.) Juss.
Orchid Family
Orchidaceae

There is beauty in simplicity, and the simple, smooth lines of this flower and plant elicit more and more admiration the longer they are studied. *Pogonia*, from the Greek meaning beard, refers to the lower lip. *Ophioglossoides* means like Ophioglossum, the Adder's Tongue Fern, and refers to the leaf shape.

The frail, fibrous roots of Rose Pogonia grow near the surface of the bog and it is from these that the plants arise. They are intolerant of drought; when bogs are disturbed or drained, the lovely little Rose Pogonia, unlike the Grass Pink which has small bulbs, perishes quickly. The simple stem has a single leaf about halfway up and a small leaf-like bract just below the flower. Although it is usually solitary, there may be as many as three flowers. The lip, which serves as a landing platform for pollinating insects, has fringed ridges with a central yellow strip.

Rose Pogonias grow in bogs and, occasionally, in wet meadows across most of Newfoundland, but not on the Northern Peninsula. They also occur west to Lake Superior and south to Florida. There are only two species of Pogonia: this one in eastern North America and *Pogonia japonica* in China and Japan. Although this species is fairly distinctive, a careful study should be made of the Dragon's Mouth (*Arethusa bulbosa* L.) and Grass Pink (*Calopogon tuberosus* (L.) BSP) so that the three are not confused.

La Scie

Dragon's Mouth

Arethusa bulbosa L.
Orchid Family
Orchidaceae

The Dragon's Mouth has a spotted tongue and yellow 'fire' in its mouth. *Arethusa* was a nymph's name and *bulbosa* means bulbous.

The stem, arising from a white or greenish bulb, bears a single leaf which often does not appear until after the flower has faded. The distinctive blossom is lovely and, like all orchids, undergoes resupination (see Small Purple Fringed Orchid).

The seeds of *Arethusa* and other orchids are remarkable, as one seed capsule usually contains hundreds of minute seeds. The seed coats are unusually thin and extend like wings at both ends. Seeds usually contain an embryo and stored food for the germinating seedling. The peanut, for example, has a papery brown seed coat and the two edible halves contain stored food (in the form of oil), which provides nutrition for young seedlings and us. One end has a tiny embryo with a stubby root and two minute leaves. The embryo of the peanut is well developed, but when an orchid seed is shed, the embryo is barely developed and has little or no stored food. In order for the embryo to survive and develop, it must become associated with one particular fungus which provides all the essential nutrients. This fungus-orchid relationship is essential for the growth of all orchids. The fungus is found near the parent orchids, which makes the seed-and-fungus association possible.

There are but two species of *Arethusa* in the world: *Arethusa bulbosa* in North America and another species in Japan. Dragon's Mouth is found on bogs all across the island except for the Northern Peninsula and north to central Labrador (Goose Bay). It also occurs in New England, the Great Lakes area, and western North Carolina. In many parts of its range it is almost extinct, but fortunately it is still abundant on many bogs in this province.

Main Brook

D.BLACK

Bakeapple

Rubus chamaemorus L.
Rose Family
Rosaceae

The bakeapple is a plant of superlatives. To overstate the case, possibly, it has the most fragile flower and a fruit with the most distinctive flavour which is the most worthy but most difficult to pick. *Rubus* is the Roman name for raspberry. It is derived from *ruber* which means red. *Chamaemorus* means ground mulberry, the old name for this plant.

A diminutive plant, it rarely exceeds 10 centimetres in height. Each plant, which bears one to three leaves, is part of a large complex of plants all linked by underground rhizomes. Recent studies have shown that all of the Bakeapples on a small bog or many of those on a larger bog may belong to the same plant. There are separate male and female plants so that a plant will produce a flower with only stamens or pistils. The fragile petals fall off with the slightest disturbance. The fruit, which are clasped by the sepals until nearly ripe, change in colour from a reddish-yellow to a translucent golden yellow.

This arctic plant has a circumpolar distribution. It occurs from Newfoundland and Labrador to Alaska, and south to northern New England and through the northern parts of the Canadian provinces from Quebec to British Columbia. In certain parts of its range, such as Scandinavia, it is called Cloudberry. Bakeapple grows in bogs and does particularly well in coastal sites. It is so distinctive that it should not be confused with any other plant. Its other relatives on the island are raspberries, plumboys, and blackberries.

The berries are often bottled and eaten with sugar and cream throughout the winter. Their distinctive flavour requires an acquired taste. It is back-breaking work to pick these berries. All too often a poor crop results from a cold period when the plant is in bloom and insect pollinators are not as active, resulting in no pollination and no fruit set. Late spring frosts are also a problem.

Baie Verte

Marshberry

Vaccinium oxycoccos L.
Heath Family
Ericaceae

This is a favourite amongst Newfoundland and Labrador's wild fruits and its fine flavour differs from its close relative, the cranberry (*Vaccinium macrocarpon* Ait.). *Vaccinium* is an ancient name which is thought to be derived from *vaccinus*, of cows. *Oxycoccos* means sour berry.

The slender and creeping Marshberry stem forms an extensive branching system occasionally reaching a length of almost one metre. The leaves are broader towards the base with their margins rolled under. Their upper surface is dark green and the lower whitened. Flowers arise from the end of the stem and, with their four upward-curved, long corolla lobes, differ markedly from most other members of the family, which have urn-shaped flowers with five short segments. There are two small bracts on each flowering stalk located below the middle of the stalk. The fruit form fairly early in the season but do not properly ripen until after the first hard frost; and those berries that overwinter have the best flavour. The berries vary in shape from oval to spherical, and are usually beige with tan spots until they ripen to a deep red with a whitish bloom.

Marshberries are found on bogs and in other moist habitats all over Newfoundland and Labrador. They grow from Greenland to Alaska and south to Washington, Michigan, and West Virginia. They also occur in Eurasia. The only other plant with which this species might be confused is the cranberry, which has similar flowers but whose bracts on the leaf stalk are larger and closer to the flower. In cranberries, leafy stems project from the point at which the flowers arise.

Cranberries are reported to be the first native North American fruit eaten in Europe. Indians cooked cranberries with maple sugar or honey. Marshberries and cranberries can be frozen or stored in water in a cool cellar. They keep well because of their acidic nature. The berries make jam, jellies, pies, fruit drinks, and other piquant treats.

La Scie

Bog Goldenrod

Solidago uliginosa Nutt.
Daisy Family
Compositae

Goldenrod, the common name of this and other species of *Solidago*, is a well-chosen name. When the leaves are removed from the stem, the rod-like stem supports the golden mass of flowers on the end. The stems are stiff and tough and can be seen rising above the snow when other herbs have been crushed by the snow. *Solidago* is from the Latin to make whole and refers to its use in healing wounds. *Uliginosa* means of marshes.

A few spatulate leaves sprawling on the sphagnum moss of a bog mark the spot where a wand of the Bog Goldenrod will rise. The stems are usually solitary and reach a height of about one metre. The basal and lower leaves are large with toothed margins, the leaves up the stem are much smaller, and the upper ones have smooth margins. The flowers are borne in a loose (as illustrated) or a broad and somewhat flattened inflorescence. The seeds are tiny cylinders with ribs along their length and a tuft of fine bristles on one end. One variety of this variable species is *terrae-novae* (of Newfoundland), a form typical of species on the island.

The Bog Goldenrod grows on bogs and peaty barrens all over the island and north to central Labrador. It occurs west to Wisconsin and south to North Carolina. Of the 12 species of *Solidago* on the island, many look the same.

Baie Verte

Stemless Plumboy

Rubus arcticus L. subsp. *acaulis* (Michx.) Foeke
Rose Family
Rosaceae

This diminutive relative of the raspberry has a richly coloured flower but it seems to get lost in the other strong colours of the bog. *Rubus*, the Roman name for these plants, is presumed to be derived from *ruber* which means red; *acaulis* means stemless.

A slender, creeping subterranean rhizome produces the frail flowering stems that rise through sphagnum moss. With the support of the moss, Stemless Plumboy appears fairly sturdy and may be from one to 10 centimetres tall. There are generally three or four leaves and a single flower, which is typical of the family, with five sepals and petals and numerous stamens. The fruit is red and similar in shape to a blackberry.

Species of *Rubus* are unusual in that they can form seeds without fertilization, a process called apomixis. Most seeds result from two parents and the resulting seedlings show variation, while seeds produced by apomixis have one parent and are clones. *Rubus* species occasionally produce seeds by sexual reproduction and these disperse to various locations. The resulting plants then produce seeds by apomixis. Each location has a large colony of a clone and these can sometimes be mistaken for different species.

Stemless Plumboys are found on bogs and in wet places on the Northern Peninsula and in a few localities in central Newfoundland. They also occur from Labrador to Alaska and south in cooler sites such as Gaspé, northern Minnesota, Saskatchewan, Colorado, and southern British Columbia.

The fruit is not plentiful in most locations, but it is reported to have a good flavour.

Crooked Bog, Gambo

Leatherleaf

Chamaedaphne calyculata (L.) Moench
Heath Family
Ericaceae

The Leatherleaf is often overlooked because it flowers so early in the spring. It does not boldly proclaim its existence by bright flowers or fruit. *Chamaedaphne* is from the Greek meaning laurel on the ground. *Calyculata* means with an outer calyx.

This evergreen shrub tends to be scraggly because it grows interspersed with other similar shrubs. The leaves are small and leathery, with tiny brownish scales on both surfaces, but more abundantly on the lower. These give the leaf its brownish leather-like appearance and, thus, its common name. The flowers hang from the new shoots in early spring and look as if they are made of thin bone china. The corolla has five small pointed lobes that flare out to give the whole flower a graceful and elegant air. A peek inside the flower reveals 10 stamens and one slender style. The small brown seed capsules split into five sections and release the numerous small seeds.

This is a shrub of wet habitats such as bogs, fens, and pond margins. It is found throughout Newfoundland and Labrador. It occurs west to Alaska and south to Wisconsin, British Columbia, and Georgia. It also grows in the northern regions of Eurasia. There are no similar species in Newfoundland and Labrador with which to confuse Leatherleaf.

The Ojibwa used this species to make tea. Leaves are collected in late winter and the tea made by steeping. Steep these leaves, but never boil, as high temperatures extract the harmful chemical andromedotoxin.

Grand Falls

Bog Rosemary

Andromeda glaucophylla Link
Heath Family
Ericaceae

The flowers of the Bog Rosemary are one of the most exquisitely coloured of any in Newfoundland and Labrador. *Andromeda* is named for the princess, Andromeda, in Greek mythology, and *glaucophylla* means with blue-green leaves.

This low shrub has stems that arch gracefully upwards. The narrow evergreen leaves are crowded towards the ends of the twigs with whitened depressed veins on the upper surface, which make them look like the leaves of the herb, Rosemary. The margins curl under and the lower surface is whitened with fine hairs. The beautiful flowers are urn-shaped. Since the flowers are pendulous, structural modifications overcome the problems of gravity. Nectar is produced to attract bees and other pollinators, and, to prevent it from running down the petals, the filaments of the stamens have a dense covering of hairs. To attract the insect's interest in the interior of the flower, nearly transparent windows in the base of the corolla light up the area of the nectar and stamens. If no insects visit the flower and effect pollination, some pollen may fall from the anthers onto the stigma. The seed capsules are five-parted and globe-shaped.

This species grows on bogs and wet heaths throughout the province and from Greenland, west to Manitoba, and south to Pennsylvania.

The leaves of Bog Rosemary may be used to make tea. It should be made by steeping, never boiling.

La Scie

Bog Laurel

Kalmia polifolia Wang.
Heath Family
Ericaceae

Although this plant is small and only produces a few flowers, its bright pink colour can be seen from some distance across the bog. *Kalmia* commemorates Linnaeus' student, Pehr Kalm (1716-1779), who travelled and collected extensively in the United States. *Polifolia* means with leaves like *Polium*, a type of germander.

Bog Laurel is a low evergreen shrub about 20 centimetres tall. The stems are smooth and have two shallow ridges. The leaves are opposite and shiny above with margins that curl under. The lower surface is whitened with small hairs. The midvein of the leaf is depressed on the upper surface but prominent on the lower surface. The saucer-shaped flowers borne at the tips of the stems may be pink or, rarely, white. Although the main blooming season is in June, the Bog Laurel often flowers late in the autumn. The flowers of this species are similar in structure and function to those of Sheep Laurel. The 10 stamens are held in little pockets of the corolla. When a flower is disturbed by an insect, the stamens are released and shower the visitor with pollen. After the stamens have been sprung, they come to rest, with the anthers in a ring around the style. The stamens are attached to the base of the corolla, and, when the corolla is released, it slips down over the style and the anthers dust the stigma with pollen. In this way pollination is ensured. The immature seed capsules are erect and bright red in colour.

This species grows in wet habitats such as bogs and fens all over Newfoundland and Labrador. It occurs west to Alaska and south to the northern United States. The other *Kalmia* in Newfoundland, Sheep Laurel, has similar flowers, but these are borne at the base of new growth. Sheep Laurel has dull leaves in threes compared to this species with its lustrous opposite leaves.

The presence of andromedotoxin in Bog Laurel makes it poisonous to humans and animals.

Baie Verte

Labrador Tea

Ledum groenlandicum Oeder
Heath Family
Ericaceae

A mention of this plant may conjure up visions of trappers in the northland sitting around a fire sipping mugs of Labrador Tea. *Ledum* is the ancient Greek name for another plant that produces an aroma similar to that of this species. *Groenlandicum* means of Greenland.

This evergreen shrub is usually less than one metre in height. New twigs are densely covered with brown hairs, while the older branches have a flaking bark. The leaves are thick and leathery, with the margins rolled under. The upper surface resembles dark green leather, and the lower surface has a dense felt of rusty hairs when mature. Young leaves have bright green hairs. These hairs are thought to be important for water conservation. The environment in the north, for which this plant is adapted, can be desert-like, with drying winds and groundwater often unavailable because of permafrost. The pores through which gaseous exchange occurs are found on the lower surface of the leaf. It is important that these pores are protected since they remain open for most of the day and water loss could be considerable. The hairs help prevent excessive water loss by creating pockets of still air under the leaf. The flowers have five to seven stamens which have hairless filaments and are followed by a 'swirl' of dry brown seed capsules that may persist for a year or more.

Labrador Tea grows on bogs, fens, heaths, and woods across Newfoundland and Labrador. It also occurs from Greenland to Alaska and south to the northern part of the United States. This is the only species of *Ledum* on the island. Northern Labrador Tea (*Ledum palustre* L.) grows in Labrador and differs in parts of the flower (10 stamens which have hairs on the filaments) and has narrow leaves. Rusty hairs on the leaves make Labrador Tea distinctive in all seasons.

To make tea, the leaves of Labrador Tea are best collected in early spring and dried. The crumbled leaves are steeped as any tea, never boiled. This tea is best served with lemon and honey.

Baie Verte

Mountain Holly

Nemopanthus mucronatus (L.) Loesner
Holly Family
Aquifoliaceae

Mountain Holly is particularly attractive when it grows on heaths and rocky barrens. Under the conditions found in these locations, the shrub is dwarfed and gnarled and the bark is a whitish-gray. It is a natural bonsai. *Nemopanthus*, from the Greek *nema*, a thread, *pous*, foot, and *anthos*, flower, refers to the slender flower stalk. *Mucronatus* means abruptly short-tipped and refers to the tips of the leaves.

This shrub can range in height from the dwarfed specimens mentioned above to one and one-half metres. The leaves usually have an untoothed margin (as illustrated), but in rare cases have teeth, and, as the species name suggests, the leaves are usually terminated by a short, sharp point. When the leaves first expand, they have a bronzy cast (as shown in the illustration), but at maturity they are a light yellowish-green. Most plants have both sexes in each flower, while a few, like corn, have separate male and female flowers. Each Mountain Holly shrub, however, has either male or female flowers. The larger branch in the illustration has male flowers, with four or five narrow petals and as many stamens as there are petals. A small nonfunctional pistil is usually present. The female shrubs have flowers with narrow petals, a functional pistil, and reduced nonfunctional stamens as shown in the lower left of the illustration. Some Mountain Holly shrubs may have both male and female flowers, and on other shrubs all flowers may have both sexes. The fruit are dull red or pale yellow with a bluish bloom and contain four or five seeds. They are not considered edible.

This species is commonly found throughout the island of Newfoundland, but less frequently on the Northern Peninsula. It usually grows in moist woods, bogs, and thickets but can also occur in exposed localities such as heaths. It is found west to Minnesota and south to west Virginia. The Holly Family has only three genera: *Ilex*, the Hollies; *Nemopanthus*, with only one species in eastern North America; and *Phelline*, with 12 species in New Caledonia. This species is not difficult to identify in flower or fruit.

Glovertown

81

Northern Honeysuckle

Lonicera villosa (Michx.) R. & S.
Honeysuckle Family
Caprifoliaceae

Late May brings the first blossoms of Northern Honeysuckle, and, although there is much to be done in that season, a walk to them is a must. The citronella-like fragrance is heavenly. *Lonicera* commemorates the sixteenth-century German herbalist, Adam Lonitzer, and *villosa* means having soft hairs.

This shrub grows up to one metre in height. The older branches have a flaky bark which comes off in strips. The dark green leaves are whitened beneath and are attached in pairs on the stem. There is considerable variation in the hairiness of the plant. The flowers and fruit are an example of siamese twins in the plant world. The Northern Honeysuckle has inferior ovaries; the flower parts are attached to the top of the ovary. Syngynia are formed by the fusion of two closely placed ovaries during the development of the flower in the bud. The dark blue berry has two eyes, formed where the flower parts were attached.

The Northern Honeysuckle grows in bogs and damp areas all over the island and north to central Labrador (Goose Bay). It extends west to the Hudson Bay area and south to Michigan and Pennsylvania. This is the only shrub on the island with double fruit.

These many-seeded fruits are usually hidden beneath the leaves and ripen in late July. The flavour is like that of a bland-tasting blueberry, and, if they can be collected in quantity, they may be eaten and used like any fruit.

Barachois Pond Provincial Park

Rhodora

Rhododendron canadense (L.) Torr.
Heath Family
Ericaceae

Rhodora is one of Newfoundland and Labrador's showiest flowering shrubs. During its blooming period it looks as if mauve clouds have descended and been caught along the edges of the forest and bogs. *Rhododendron* is a Greek name meaning rose tree and *canadense* means Canadian.

This shrub can reach a height of one metre. The leaves do not unfold completely until the flowers have opened, so it is often difficult to associate the two phases of one plant. The leaves have their margins rolled under and pointed at both ends. They are greyish-green and covered with hairs. Rhodora blooms in June and it is difficult, if not impossible, to capture the profusion of colour correctly on film. As pollinating insects are often not abundant in the spring, pollination may not occur. In order to ensure production of seeds, Rhodora uses its corolla. The corolla has separate segments fused into a tube at the base. After the flower has been open for several days, the entire corolla slips down the filaments of the stamens and brings the anthers into contact with the stigma, so that pollination is effected. Many minute seeds are borne in the hairy capsules and dispersed by the wind in the fall. Their flattened, wing-like seed coat aids in their dispersal.

This species occurs in most areas of Newfoundland and north to southern Labrador, the Maritimes, and New England. The other species found in Newfoundland and Labrador, Lapland Rosebay (*Rhododendron lapponicum* (L.) Wahlenb.), is evergreen and has magenta-coloured flowers. Rhodora grows on bogs, heaths, around clearings in woods, and around ponds.

Chuckley Pear and Rhodora produce abundant bloom in June. They are but two of the many wildflowers that make the roadside and countryside a flower garden for all to enjoy.

Baie Verte

85

Shrubby Cinquefoil

Potentilla fruticosa L.
Rose Family
Rosaceae

This plant is unusual because it is not common to have single large flowers on a shrub, particularly yellow flowers. Clusters of flowers are more common. *Potentilla* comes from *potens*, which means powerful and this refers to Silverweed (*Potentilla anserina* L.) which was once considered to have powerful medicinal qualities. *Fruticosa* means shrubby.

Shrubby Cinquefoil can form a dense shrub although it also can be straggly. The reddish-brown bark of the older branches is shredded into greyish strips and the newer branches are light reddish-brown, with a dense covering of hairs. The pinnate compound leaves usually have five sharp-pointed leaflets, although some leaves may have seven. The margins of the leaflets are untoothed and rolled under. Both surfaces have silky white hairs, but the undersurface is densely hairy and whitened.

The bright yellow flowers are borne singly or occur in clusters of three or four but with only one flower opening at a time. Flowers appear over a long period, from early July until mid-September. The fruit consists of many small seeds in a capsule enclosed by the tough calyx. When the seeds mature, the calyx opens up to a saucer shape and the seeds are gradually dispersed. The calyx often persists until the following year; identification of the shrub is fairly simple even when no leaves are present.

This is the only woody species of *Potentilla* in Newfoundland and Labrador. It is distinctive, so identification should not be difficult. It grows most frequently in wet places such as the shores of ponds and brooks, fens, roadsides, and moist areas by the forest's edge. It occurs throughout Newfoundland and north to central Labrador. It is found west to Alaska, south to New Jersey in the east, and California in the west, and also grows in Eurasia.

The leaves of Shrubby Cinquefoil may be used as a substitute for tea and in folk medicine they have been used to treat diarrhea. Many cultivars for gardens are available from nurseries.

Baie Verte

Bartram's Chuckley Pear

Amelanchier bartramiana (Tausch) Roemer
Rose Family
Rosaceae

This is a local representative of the Saskatoon-berry, the premier fruit of the Prairies. It is a lovely shrub throughout the entire growing season. *Amelanchier* is the Provençal name for a European species of this genus. *Bartramiana* commemorates William Bartram (1739-1823), who sent seeds from North America to European gardens.

This moderate-sized shrub has oval leaves with finely toothed margins. The overwintering buds are long and slender with many bud scales that have hairy margins. Each inflorescence has one to three flowers, which separates it from the other five species on the island.

Bartram's Chuckley Pear grows in thickets, edges of woods, and roadsides across Newfoundland and Labrador, west to Ontario, and south to Pennsylvania. This is the only species in Labrador.

Amelanchier species are called Pear Tree, Indian Pear, and Wild Pear in this province, and Juneberry, Sugarplum, Shadbush, Serviceberry, and Sarviceberry in other areas of eastern North America. It is used in baking and jam making.

Baie Verte

Virginian Rose

Rosa virginiana Mill.
Rose Family
Rosaceae

In spite of its bristles and prickles, the rose holds a special place in many people's minds. Pick a wild rose bud in the evening and put it in a vase to enjoy its perfume at breakfast. *Rosa* is its ancient Latin name and *virginiana* means Virginian.

This species forms a dense shrub up to one metre in height. The canes of Virginian Rose have scattered prickles and compound leaves that turn red or orange in the autumn. The leaflets are toothed on the upper three-quarters of the margin. Its large, attractive flowers last for only a single day. Abundant pollen is provided in the numerous stamens for visiting insects but no nectar is present. The perfume, which attracts bees and other insects, is an alcoholic derivative of paraffin. The fruit of the rose, called a hip, is an interesting structure consisting of an orange, fleshy outer portion that encloses seeds embedded in dense hairs. The five sepals remain attached to the top. The fleshy section is thought to be derived from a modification of the tip of the flower stalk and the bases of the sepals and petals. It is a false fruit since a true fruit is technically derived from just the ovary. In this case only the seeds are derived from the ovaries and so they are the true fruit.

The Virginian Rose is found on fens, along streams, and in other damp habitats in most of Newfoundland except the Northern Peninsula. It is found west to southern Ontario and south to the southeastern United States. New canes of the Northeastern Rose (*Rosa nitida* Willd.), which also grows in Newfoundland, are densely covered with dark red bristles and a few prickles.

Wild Rose petals are collected to make jelly or rose water, or candied. The hips make a good jelly, jam, or tea. Vitamin-C-rich rose hips provide an excellent supplement to the winter diets of people and animals.

Hare Bay

Hooded Lady's-tresses

Spiranthes romanzoffiana Cham.
Orchid Family
Orchidaceae

While Russia still ruled Alaska, Adalbert von Chamisso discovered this species on the Aleutian Island of Unalaska and named it in honour of his patron, Nicholas Romanzoff, a Russian minister of state. *Spiranthes* means coiled flowers and refers to the twisted spike. *Romanzoffiana* is named for Count Romanzoff (1754-1826).

This plant, which usually grows to a height of about 20 centimetres, has long fleshy roots grouped like a bunch of bananas. There are three to six leaves along the stem. Up to 60 flowers are crowded in the spike and appear to be in three spirals. This is the derivation of its common name of Lady's-tresses, tresses being a traditional name for braids. Each flower has a green bract associated with it. The flowers exude an almond-like fragrance which attracts insects to alight on the curved lip and feed on the nectar and hairs present in the throat. The hairs are rich in fat and protein, and the nectar contains sugars. The seed capsule is dry and elliptical in outline and disperses thousands of tiny seeds when it breaks open.

The Hooded Lady's-tresses has a curious geographical distribution. It occurs in eastern Siberia, from Alaska to Newfoundland and Labrador, with extensions south to California in the Rocky Mountains and just south of the Great Lakes. It also grows in Ireland and the islands of Colonsay and Coll in the Hebrides. It grows across Newfoundland and north to central Labrador in meadows, clearings in the woods, along shrubbery, and in grassy areas on roadsides. It seems to grow where orchids are not expected. This species is the only orchid in Newfoundland with a tightly spiralled inflorescence and almond-like fragrance.

Baie Verte

Spreading Dogbane

Apocynum androsaemifolium L.
Dogbane Family
Apocynaceae

Spreading Dogbane is conspicuous late into autumn; although the plant's stiff stems may remain bare, it still has long, slender dangling seed capsules. *Apocynum* is a former name for a related plant in Europe known as Dogbane and means far from a dog. *Androsaemifolium* means that the leaves resemble those of *Androsaemum*.

This species looks different from many of the plants in this province because of its plain leaves. The leaves are fairly smooth, have an untoothed margin, and are opposite. The plant grows up to 50 centimetres in height. Each bell-shaped flower produces two long, slender, shiny dark brown fruit capsules.

The Spreading Dogbane is one of three similar species of *Apocynum* found in central and western Newfoundland. This species grows in the shrubbery at the edges of woods from Newfoundland to Alaska and south to northern Mexico and east to West Virginia.

The common name, Dogbane, suggests that dogs avoid this plant. It is distasteful, even poisonous, to animals. Chemicals which affect the heart have been extracted from the plant.

South Brook

Twisted-stalk

Streptopus amplexifolius (L.) DC.
Lily Family
Liliaceae

The exotic-looking Twisted-stalk is a pleasure to find in the woods. *Streptopus*, meaning twisted stalk, refers to the flower's stalk which is twisted in some species. *Amplexifolius* means clasping leafed.

The stout stems arising from a short, creeping rhizome grow to a height of 80 centimetres, and usually branch. The leaves have heart-shaped bases which tend to clasp and extend part of the way around the stem. The veins of the leaves are parallel to each other and extend the length of the leaf blade. Monocots, a large group of flowering plants, characteristically have flower parts in threes or multiples of three. Twisted-stalk has six tepals, six stamens, and three stigmas. The berries are scarlet in colour, elliptical in shape, and many-seeded. The colour of the berry has given rise to the common name Liverberry.

Twisted-stalk is not common, but has been reported in woods all over the island and Labrador. This species occurs in Europe and in the northern parts of the United States and all of Canada. It also extends down the Rocky Mountains to Arizona. There is another species on the island part of this province which differs in the shape of the base of the leaf and the stigma.

This elegant plant is especially attractive when it is in fruit. The edible berries have a slight cucumber flavour. Care should be taken that not too many are eaten as they are cathartic.

Baie Verte

97

Water Avens

Geum rivale L.
Rose Family
Rosaceae

The hairiness of the Water Avens gives it a soft appearance. With the subtle contrast of the colours of the sepals and petals, the flowers also appear delicate. *Geum* is a name Pliny used for these plants, and *rivale* means of brook sides.

This plant can reach a height of almost one metre. The basal leaves are compound but not as distinctly compound as those of a rose or dogberry. The terminal leaflets are large and not always completely separate, while the lower leaflets are small. The flowers are borne at the ends of the branches and, while they are open, they nod. The flower stalk straightens by the time the fruit matures. The fruit of this and some other *Geum* species have an effective dispersal mechanism. The style is sharply hooked below the stigma, and after flowering, when the stigma has dropped off, the style becomes woody and the hook sharp. The hook catches any passing fur, feather, or cloth and can be transported for some distance.

This species grows in wet meadows, woods, and similar habitats in Eurasia, throughout Newfoundland and Labrador, most of Canada, and much of the northeastern United States. Two other species in Newfoundland and Labrador that feature upward-facing yellow flowers are the Yellow Avens (*Geum aleppicum* Jacq.) and the Large-leafed Avens (*Geum macrophyllum* Willd.).

Another name for Water Avens is Chocolate-root and, as the name implies, the root is used to make a chocolate-flavoured drink. The roots are boiled well and sugar is added. This root, used in the Middle Ages, was steeped in wine in the spring and then drunk early in the morning to "comfort the heart" and protect it from vapours and poisons.

Baie Verte

Northern Wild Raisin

Viburnum cassinoides L.
Honeysuckle Family
Caprifoliaceae

The Northern Wild Raisin is a shrub for all seasons. Its scurfy rust-coloured buds are easily distinguishable in winter and unroll into leaves and flowers in the spring. The fruit change through a series of colours during the summer, and in the autumn the leaves turn scarlet, contrasting well with the dark blue fruit. *Viburnum*, a name of doubtful meaning, is the classical Latin name of these plants. *Cassinoides* means like *Ilex cassine*, a holly.

Northern Wild Raisin is usually about two metres tall, but it can range from one to three metres. It is considerably branched and the young shoots are covered with rust-coloured scales. In the winter there are opposite buds along the twigs. The buds that develop into leafy branches are long and narrow, while those that produce flowers have a swollen base and are borne on the ends of the branches. The leaves are opposite and shiny with a toothless or variously toothed margin. A narrow wing of the leaf blade often extends down the petiole. In autumn, the leaves turn purplish, then scarlet.

The white flowers are borne in flat-topped clusters. The elongated fruit change in colour from yellowish-white to rose-tinged to dark blue with a white bloom. Potentially, each fruit has four seeds, but three of the ovules abort and only one large flat seed develops.

Northern Wild Raisin grows in moist habitats such as clearings, edges of woods, wet heaths, and thickets along streams and around ponds. It is common throughout most of Newfoundland, but it is rare on the Northern Peninsula. It occurs west to Ontario and south to Tennessee.

The fruit makes a drink that tastes like prune juice and has a similar effect.

Trout River

101

Red Elderberry

Sambucus pubens Michx.
Honeysuckle Family
Caprifoliaceae

The fruit of the Red Elderberry is one of the brightest and most conspicuous in Newfoundland. They are especially attractive when viewed from below against a blue sky. *Sambucus* is from the Greek *sambuce*, an ancient musical instrument. This shrub has easily removed bark and has been used to make flutes and whistles. *Pubens* means pubescent and refers to the hairy twigs.

This shrub grows to a height of about four metres. The opposite compound leaves are dark green above and paler with hairs beneath. They give off a foul odour when bruised. As branches get older, the colour of the bark changes. Twigs are light brown and hairy. Older branches have smooth brown bark with warty lenticels. The flowers are borne in pyramidal clusters and are small individually but conspicuous as a group. The petals are usually creamy white but they can be pink. Many flowers attract insect pollinators by providing nectar, but the Red Elderberry is visited for its abundant protein-rich pollen, used by bees as their chief protein ration for brood-rearing. Red Elderberry and other so-called pollen flowers produce enough food for bees and for pollination. In this plant, the problem of rapid pollen spoilage due to dampness is avoided as the anthers open only in dry weather.

The Red Elderberry grows along roadsides and in open places in the woods. It grows west of Clarenville in central and western parts of the island. It occurs from Newfoundland to Alaska and south to Colorado and Georgia. The other Elder in Newfoundland is the European Elder, which has black fruit.

The fruit of Red Elderberry is inedible because the plant contains poisonous substances. Animals have been poisoned by its roots, leaves, and stems, and children have become sick after using Elder stems for blow-guns or whistles.

Baie Verte

Pin Cherry

Prunus pensylvanica L.f.
Rose Family
Rosaceae

Pin Cherries are one of the most colourful trees of Newfoundland and Labrador in the autumn. The lower and thus inner leaves on each branch turn crimson first, and this makes the whole tree look as if it were glowing like a live coal. *Prunus* is the ancient Latin name for the plum, another member of this genus, and *pensylvanica* means Pennsylvanian.

This small tree is usually less than eight metres in height. It often has a rounded crown, made up of slender twigs with leaves dripping from their ends. The bark of the main trunk and branches is a bronzy-brown, while that of the older parts of the trunk is grey. The flowers are typical of members of the Rose Family: they have five sepals, five petals, and many stamens. Abundant nectar is provided for insect visitors. The fruit mature during the latter half of August. A thin, sour layer of scarlet flesh covers the large stone. This is a good example of the type of fruit known as a drupe.

This species occurs commonly in Newfoundland and north to central Labrador. It is also found west to British Columbia and south to Tennessee and Colorado. It is an important colonizer of areas where the forest has been removed by fire or cutting. Since it is such a dominant plant on burnt-over areas, it is frequently known as Fire Cherry. It also grows along rivers, ponds, and edges of forests, forming thickets. The other species of Prunus in Newfoundland, the Chokecherry (*Prunus virginiana* L.), has pendulous fingers of black fruit.

The fruit are used for making jelly, but the rest of the plant is poisonous and has been responsible for the death of domestic animals. The leaves contain hydrogen cyanide and, once injested, death soon follows. The leaves do, however, have a lower concentration of hydrogen cyanide in the autumn. As the stones also contain this lethal substance, they should not be swallowed or used to obtain a second batch of jelly from the same fruit.

Baie Verte

Chokecherry

Prunus virginiana L.
Rose Family
Rosaceae

Chokecherries are rewarding fruit to pick, as they do not require the endless individual attention involved in filling a bucket with other fruit. Just hold a bucket underneath and pull the berries from the heavy, dropping clusters. *Prunus* is the ancient Latin name of the plum, another member of this genus, and *virginiana* means Virginian.

This large shrub or small tree often grows in clumps. The bark is grey to reddish in colour. The leaves are much broader than those of the other species in the province, the Pin Cherry (*Prunus pensylvanica* L.f.), and they tend to be broader towards the tip and then abruptly pointed. The margin has numerous sharp teeth, ending in hair-like points.

The flowers, borne in cylindrical clusters that may vary from erect to arching to drooping, are typical of the Rose Family, with five sepals and five white petals. White is a common colour for petals in this family, although some some members of the family have pink and others yellow. There are many stamens in the flowers of most of this family and this species has 20. Delicious fruit are also common in the Rose Family: apples, plums, cherries, strawberries, raspberries, blackberries, pears, quinces, prunes, peaches, apricots, almonds, nectarines, loquats, and loganberries. Chokecherries are dark purplish or almost black when ripe and contain a single large seed. They usually ripen by early September.

This species is mainly found in the rich moist soils of stream banks, roadsides, and forest edges throughout Newfoundland, with the exception of the Northern Peninsula, and north to central Labrador. It also occurs west to British Columbia and south to Tennessee.

The fruit are astringent; a few berries dry out the mouth and make whistling difficult. Despite the nature of the raw fruit, they make a delicious jelly on their own or mixed with apple. It is not advisable to boil the seeds of this or any cherry a second time as they contain poisonous hydrogen cyanide. Aboriginal peoples made a paste from the fruit, which they dried and added to pemmican. A drink can also be prepared from the juice. The leaves contain fairly large quantities of hydrogen cyanide and the concentration increases when they wilt. Because of their poisonous nature the leaves should not be fed to animals.

Baie Verte

Northern Dogberry

Sorbus decora (Sarg.) Schneid.
Rose Family
Rosaceae

The Northern Dogberry crop is carefully watched in late summer to determine whether winter will be severe. An abundant crop is said to herald a harsh winter, while the opposite is also believed to be true. *Sorbus* is the ancient Latin name of a European species. *Americana* means American.

These small trees range in height from three to six metres, with a short trunk and many ascending branches that form a rounded crown. The twigs are reddish-brown and later grey. The bark of the main branches and trunk is grey with large horizontal, warty lenticels. Lenticels are areas of corky tissue that allow the passage of air and thus the exchange of gases across the bark, which is an otherwise impervious layer. This gas exchange is necessary for the functioning of the cells in the trunk responsible for the transport of water, nutrients, and manufactured food, and for the formation of more wood and bark.

Each compound leaf has from 11 to 17 leaflets, which are shiny green above and paler below. The flowers have five sepals, five white petals, and the many stamens typical of the Rose Family. The large clusters of bright orange-red to scarlet fruit often persist through the winter.

This species is found throughout Newfoundland and north to central Labrador in open woods, thickets, and similar habitats. It is more common than the other native species, the American Dogberry (*Sorbus americana* Marsh). The European Mountain Ash (*Sorbus aucuparia* L.), which can be confused with the two native species, is commonly found around some settlements. The Northern Dogberry occurs in southern Greenland, west to Manitoba, and south to New York.

The flavour of the berries improves after a light frost, but it may not always be possible to find them then. In some parts of Europe the berries are dried and ground into flour, tasty in cookies or quick breads, or used to make a pleasant and potent wine. Overwintering robins eat much of the fruit.

Baie Verte

Squashberry

Viburnum edule (Michx.) Raf.
Honeysuckle
Caprifoliaceae

Squashberry fills another shelf of nature's larder. In many locations, the fruit can be picked in sufficient quantity to make jelly. *Viburnum* is the classical Latin name (meaning is unknown) and *edule* means edible.

These short shrubs grow in open woods. They have opposite leaves and clusters of flowers along the stem. The fruit are a lovely, translucent orange-red. Only one seed is produced per fruit; the others abort. The large seed has a different type of germination pattern. In autumn, when the seed has landed on the ground, it germinates by producing a hypocotyl, which produces a seedling root system that replaces the initial root system. Then germination stops because of epicotyl dormancy. The epicotyl is the seedling shoot which produces the above-ground portion of the plant. In this case, the epicotyl must be chilled for two to three months before it develops. Epicotyl dormancy also occurs in other large seeds such as those of lilies and peonies. This mechanism, presumably, anchors the seed so it is not washed away over the winter; germination then continues in the spring.

Squashberry grows throughout the province, west to Alaska and Oregon, and south to Colorado and Pennsylvania. The fruit are enjoyed fresh or cooked.

Baie Verte

Highbush Cranberry

Viburnum trilobum Marsh.
Honeysuckle Family
Caprifoliaceae

With its crisp lines and sharp colours, Highbush Cranberry is a tall fashionably tailored shrub. *Viburnum* is the name given in the Middle Ages to these plants, and *trilobum* means three-lobed.

The leaves of these tall shrubs, or in some locations, small trees, are a rich, deep green, often with a thin red edge. The overwintering buds are stout and angular, with the two outer scales fused along their margins. In order to ensure pollination, flowers must be noticeable to insects. Since small flowers require less energy to produce, plants tend to produce smaller blooms rather than large flowers such as roses. Small flowers are noticeable if clustered together as in the Squashberry, which are grouped into large masses so as to be noticeable to pollinating insects. In Highbush Cranberry, the cluster is ringed by sterile flowers with broad, flat corollas. The fruit mature late in the autumn and have a single flat seed.

Highbush Cranberry is found across the island of Newfoundland, west to British Columbia, south to Washington in the west, and south to Pennsylvania in the east.

The fruit make a delicious sauce or jelly when the seeds are sieved out.

Lomond

Skunk Currant

Ribes glandulosum Grauer
Saxifrage Family
Saxifragaceae

The Skunk Currant is a plant of contrasts. It has a distinctly skunky smell, often grows best in piles of tin cans and other rubbish, and yet produces a pleasant jelly. *Ribes* is reputedly derived from *ribs*, an archaic Danish name for Red Currant. *Glandulosum* means glandular and refers to the plant's glandular hairs.

This shrub derives its common name from the odour emitted when its leaves or fruit are crushed. This fragrance is produced by glandular hairs, which are hairs that have bulbous glands on their tips. The purpose of the musky oil produced by these glands is unknown. Glandular hairs are found on the bases of the leaves and on most of the inflorescence and bright red fruit. The leaves are shaped like those of maple, and turn a brilliant scarlet in the autumn. The petals of the flowers vary in colour from white to pink and often change colour with age. The flowers occur in pendulous spikes and open early in the season. Nectar, produced in the base of the flower, is protected from theft by small insects by numerous stiff hairs on the style. Insects are thieves when they take nectar but do not pollinate the flower, usually because they are too small to do so.

Skunk Currant, the most common currant in Newfoundland and Labrador, is found in damp woods, clearings, and other moist, shady habitats. It also occurs west to northern British Columbia and south to the mountains of North Carolina. There are three other native currants but only this one has red berries covered with glandular hairs.

The fruit, often found in fairly large quantities, make a fine jelly without any skunky odour.

Baie Verte

Bristly Black Currant

Ribes lacustre (Pers.) Poir.
Saxifrage Family
Saxifragaceae

Native currants rarely grow dense enough to produce an abundance of fruit. *Ribes* likely comes from the Danish word, *ribs*, for Red Currant and *lacustre* means of lakes.

The leaf of this species is more lacy than that of the garden variety, the young stems are bristly and have weak thorns, and the berries are bristly. Plant hairs, called trichomes, are elongated extensions of epidermal cells and can form on any part of the plant. Bristles and prickles are particularly well-developed forms of trichomes.

This species grows in central and western Newfoundland, north to central Labrador, west to Alaska, and south to California in the west, and Tennessee in the east.

The fruit make tasty jam and preserves. Members of the genus, *Ribes*, which include currants and gooseberries, were outlawed and destroyed in the earlier part of the twentieth century, as they were hosts of the White Pine Blister Rust which killed much of this important timber species. There are two native pines in the province, White Pine and Red Pine, but most of the White Pines were lost during the rust outbreak. Similar wheat rusts are a potential problem in agriculture with the alternate host being barberry, which is eradicated in wheat-growing areas.

Baie Verte

Showy Lady's-slipper

Cypripedium reginae Walt.
Orchid Family
Orchidaceae

Slippers for the mythical faerie queen are produced each summer in the woods of the island of Newfoundland by plants of the Showy Lady's-slipper. *Cypripedium* is from the Greek – *Kypris*, goddess of love and beauty, and *pedilon* meaning slipper. *Reginae* means of the queen.

The Showy Lady's-slipper has large bright green leaves that are hairy and pleated, and which give a lush appearance to open spots in the woods where they grow. The leaves and flowering stalk arise from a stout rhizome, and the plant ranges from 30 to 50 centimetres in height. The petals are glistening white and the pouched lip varies from pale to deep pink or occasionally white. The structure protruding into the pouch is a gynostemium, which is white with yellow patches that have red spots and consists of the stamens and style, which have fused together. This flower is an example of a pitfall flower; flies and small bees are attracted to it by the colour of its blossom and the scent of its nectar. The insect creeps into the pouch, eats some of the nectar, and then tries to leave. Although there are several ways for an insect to fall into the pouch, because of the curvature of the walls there is only one way out. The insect brushes past the stigma, where pollen from a previously visited flower may be deposited, and then pushes its way through one of the openings at the base of the flower. As it squeezes out, the insect, smeared with pollen from the anthers, is now ready to visit the next flower.

This lovely plant is found in open sites with damp calcareous soil from White Bay to Cape St. George. Its range extends west to Manitoba and south through the mountains to north Georgia. There are two other species, the yellow *Cypripedium calceolus* and the pink *Cypripedium acaule*.

This flower should be admired by all and left for everyone. Do not try to transplant it, as most of this province's soils are unsuitable. Touching the leaves may cause a severe skin rash.

Gros Morne National Park

Wild Lily-of-the-Valley

Maianthemum canadense Desf.
Lily Family
Liliaceae

Some plants have two common names: one when the plant is in blossom, the other when it is in fruit. This species is called Wild Lily-of-the-Valley, Mayflower, or Two-leafed Solomon's Seal in the spring, and Catberry in the autumn; but, by whatever name it is known, it is beautiful. *Maianthemum* is Latin for mayflower and *canadense* means Canadian.

The thread-like rhizomes branch freely and creep below the surface of the moss or soil. They produce stalked tuberous enlargements at intervals along their length. A single broad leaf will frequently appear in a year when a plant does not flower. When an inflorescence is produced, there are usually two leaves on the stem, although this varies from one to three. The bases of the leaves clasp the stem, as seen in the illustration.

The sweetly fragrant flowers are borne in a terminal cylindrical cluster. These are unusual for members of the Lily Family as they have parts in fours – four tepals and four stamens. The Lily Family usually has its parts in threes or sixes. This flower is obviously the product of reduction. The berries in the illustration are in the unripe, speckled stage. When the berries are fully ripe, they are translucent crimson and contain one or two seeds.

Wild Lily-of-the-Valley is found in woods and clearings in the woods as well as on seaside heaths and subalpine hilltops. It may not always be in flower, but the single distinctive leaf is visible. It is found across Newfoundland and Labrador, west to northern British Columbia, and south to North Carolina.

The bittersweet berries are cathartic and should be eaten with caution.

Baie Verte

One-sided Pyrola

Pyrola secunda L.
Wintergreen Family
Pyrolaceae

This plant is a reminder that spruce and fir forests are a part of the greater boreal forest that stretches from sea to sea. The One-sided Pyrola is common throughout this vegetation zone. *Pyrola* means little pear tree, *secunda* one-sided.

The shiny, dark green leaves are scattered on the stem, and the evergreen nature of the leaves means that the plant is ever-present on the forest floor. The leaves form an irregular rosette and the plant barely emerges above the moss. The flowers, located along one side of the flower stalk and give rise to its species name, are like little greenish-white lamp shades with dangling switch strings. The petals have ragged margins and the protruding style has a five-lobed stigma. The anthers are distinctive in that the pollen is released through end pores instead of splitting along their length, as is the case in most flowers. The seed capsule, flattened and brown at maturity, often remains on the plant for some time.

This species is found in woods across the island of Newfoundland, north to northern Labrador (Hebron), and west to Alaska. It occurs south to Virginia, Indiana, and California, and also in Eurasia. There are six other species on the island, but none has flowers on one side of the stalk.

In medieval rural England, the leaves of pyrolas were used in poultices applied to bruises. North American Aboriginals and early colonists used pyrolas for rheumatism, coughs, and cankers.

Baie Verte

Lesser Rattlesnake Plantain

Goodyera repens (L.) R.Br.
Orchid Family
Orchidaceae

With its stalks of snowy flowers rising from whorls of checkered leaves clustered on the mossy forest floor, this plant ranks higher in beauty with each session of study and admiration. *Goodyera* commemorates English botanist John Goodyer (1592-1664). *Repens* means creeping.

This is the smallest member of the genus in North America. It consists of a rhizome that spreads horizontally in the damp humus of the forest floor, producing a few roots and occasionally branching. The growing tip of the rhizome produces a whorl of evergreen leaves that are a dark bluish-green with a pattern of silvery-white. The leaves vary markedly in their patterns. Investigations have shown that the rosette of leaves is not produced until the fifth year from seed and the flower spike not until the eighth year. After a rosette has flowered, it dies, and those of other younger branches flower another year. The flower spike is slender and covered with a down of fine hairs. It shows little variation in form throughout its range in the Northern Hemisphere. A single file of dainty white flowers, which may be pink-tinged, tends to be on one side of the stalk. The lip of the flower is sack-shaped and ends in a curving spout.

The Lesser Rattlesnake Plantain is found in damp, mossy coniferous forests across the island of Newfoundland and north to central Labrador. It also occurs across Canada, into Alaska, and throughout the Soviet Union and most of Europe. The Tessellated Rattlesnake Plantain (*Goodyera tesselata* Lodd.) also grows on the island.

The origin of the common name of these orchids, Rattlesnake Plantain, is particularly interesting. Plantain is from the Latin *planta*, meaning the sole of the foot, and is used for several plants with broad flat leaves. The reticulate marks on the leaves, reminiscent of the patterns on snakes, was one reason some aboriginal peoples used this plant for snake bites. They are reported to have carried rhizomes with them and when bitten by a snake, chewed some, and after swallowing them, applied more rhizomes to the wound.

Barachois Pond Provincial Park

Pink Pyrola

Pyrola asarifolia Michx.
Wintergreen Family
Pyrolaceae

These round, leathery leaves scattered in little groups across the forest floor appear purposeless, as they seem destined to become something larger – a shrub or even a tree. In flower, however, most would agree that they need not aspire to become any more than they are. *Pyrola* means little pear tree and refers to the resemblance of the leaves of some species to those of pears. *Asarifolia* means with the leaves of *Asarum*, the Wild Ginger of central North America.

Pink Pyrolas have extensively creeping underground rhizomes that produce loose rosettes of leaves. The round evergreen leaves with their heart-shaped bases are leathery in texture and dull on the upper surface. The internal structure of the leaves of Pyrolas and other evergreen plants differ from that of deciduous trees and shrubs. The chlorophyll-filled cells of a leaf, where photosynthesis occurs, are called palisade cells and are arranged in one or more layers just below the surface. Within the leaves of deciduous woody plants that develop in full sunlight, there are two or three layers of palisade cells, which take full advantage of the radiant energy of the sun. In the leaves of shrubs growing in the shade or in leaves found within the shady crown of a tree, there is only one layer of palisade cells. Evergreen plants such as Pyrola, Partridgeberry, and Holly, on the other hand, produce leaves with comparatively well-developed layers of palisade cells, even in the shadiest locations.

This species, which grows in the woods of central and western Newfoundland as well as the Northern Peninsula and north to southern Labrador, prefers rich calcareous sites. It also occurs west to Alaska, south to New York in the east, and New Mexico in the west.

Beothuk Park

Twinflower

Linnaea borealis L.
Honeysuckle Family
Caprifoliaceae

With its sweetly perfumed, delicate flowers and its soft vines spreading across a carpet of moss, this is one of the daintiest flowers of the forest floor. *Linnaea* is named for Carolus Linnaeus (1707-1778), father of modern taxonomy, and *borealis* means northern.

Because the Twinflower's slender trailing stems are slightly woody and its leaves evergreen, some consider this plant a shrub or a sub-shrub. The stems are hairy and may be green or dark red. The broad opposite leaves have a few teeth towards the tip and hairs scattered over both surfaces. The common name of Twinflower is easily understood, as all of the flowers are in pairs. On rare occasions – much rarer than a four-leafed clover – flowers in quadruplets have been found. The corollas of Twinflower, which may be evenly suffused with pink or white and tinged and striped with deep rose, are hairy inside. They bloom from late June to early August.

Of the four stamens in each flower, two are shorter, thus reiterating the theme of twins. The fruit is a small one-seeded dry capsule enclosed by the calyx. The calyx has numerous glandular hairs that exude a sticky fluid that helps the calyx and fruit adhere firmly to passing animals, birds, and people.

Twinflower grows mostly in our coniferous forests but also ventures onto heaths, fens, and barrens throughout Newfoundland and north to northern Labrador (Okak). It occurs from western Greenland to Alaska and south to West Virginia in the east and California in the west. It also grows in northern Eurasia.

Twinflowers were a favourite of Linnaeus and a portrait of him shows him holding a small flowering branch. He put order into the chaos of Latin names for plants in his 1753 book, *Species Plantarum*, the starting point for all modern botanical names.

River of Ponds

Hairy Plumboy

Rubus pubescens Raf.
Rose Family
Rosaceae

The fruit of this species are much more flavourful than blackberries. *Rubus*, the Roman name, is probably related to *ruber*, which means red. *Pubescens* means hairy.

The stem is slender and trails across the forest floor, with an occasional ascending branch. The leaves are like a tender version of the raspberry leaf and the flowers are similar to raspberry flowers. The nectar provided in the flower is concealed amongst the bases of the flower structures, but members of this genus have abandoned a dependence on pollination. They have resorted to apogamy, where an ovule develops into a viable seed without fertilization. Apogamy, a form of apomixis, ensures seed production even under poor conditions. The Hairy Plumboy has an aggregate fruit of many drupelets attached to a spongy receptacle.

The Hairy Plumboy grows throughout Newfoundland and Labrador, west to British Columbia, and south to Colorado in the west and Pennsylvania in the east.

The fruit make tasty jam, desserts, and garnishes.

Baie Verte

Clintonia

Clintonia borealis (Ait.) Raf.
Lily Family
Liliaceae

Clintonia has common names that change with the seasons. It is often called Corn Lily in the spring when it is in bloom and Bluebead Lily in the autumn when it bears fruit. *Clintonia* commemorates De Witt Clinton (1769-1828), a governor of New York, and *borealis* means northern.

The two to four glossy, olive-green leaves may grow up to 20 centimetres long. The slender flowering stalk arises from the centre of the rosette of leaves and bears two to eight flowers on its tip. The greenish-yellow tepals, which are downy on the outside, lend the plant its common name, Corn Lily. The fruit, a dark metallic blue berry, is displayed in clusters on tall stalks. Although a white-coloured berry has been reported, it has not yet been seen in Newfoundland.

This species is northern in distribution. It grows in rich moist woods and even into subalpine meadows all over the island of Newfoundland and north to central Labrador. It is found from Labrador to Manitoba, south to Michigan, and through the mountains to Georgia. Clintonia might be confused with Pink Lady's-slipper, which has duller, hairy leaves.

The young, just unrolling leaves of Clintonia are used in salads or steamed like turnip greens. The berries are considered to be poisonous, although no actual cases of poisoning have been reported. Since their edibility is doubtful, they should be avoided.

Baie Verte

Trailing Arbutus

Epigaea repens L.
Heath Family
Ericaceae

The Trailing Arbutus lit by the delicate light of spring is a study in pastels reposing on the forest floor. It may be found blooming early in the spring, even peeping through the snow. *Epigaea* means upon the earth and *repens* means creeping.

This evergreen shrub, as the Latin name suggests, is prostrate and can form extensive patches. The leaves are leathery and both surfaces are shiny, with a few hairs. The margins and petioles are hairy. The fragrant flowers are pink or white, with a corolla which has a short tube and a flat, five-lobed portion that is the most evident part of the flower. The Trailing Arbutus is intermediate between plants that have stamens and pistils in each flower and other plants which have separate male and female flowers either on the same or different plants. It has two types of flowers. The first type has a pistil with a stigma that gets sticky so that pollen adheres to it. There are usually only sterile stamen filaments, and pollen is rarely produced. Seed is produced in these flowers. The second type has a pistil of normal appearance but the stigma never gets sticky. The stamens, however, are fully functional. Seeds are never produced. These flowers, therefore, look as if they have both sexes in each flower, but they do not function that way.

This species is found in certain localities of central and western Newfoundland and north to southern Labrador. It grows on forest floors, boggy barrens, and limestone ledges. Its range extends west to Saskatchewan and south to Tennessee.

The flowers of Trailing Arbutus have a lovely spicy fragrance. When the flowers are nibbled, the juice has a slightly acidic, spicy flavour.

Corner Brook

Naked Mitrewort

Mitella nuda L.
Saxifrage Family
Saxifragaceae

When they are not in flower, it would be easy to overlook the little green leaves of the Naked Mitrewort on the forest floor, but, when it blooms, the plant is fascinating. *Mitella* is from *mitra*, a cap, and alludes to the shape of the young fruit. *Nuda* means naked and refers to the leafless flower stalk.

The shape of the leaves of this species is similar to that of many members of the Saxifrage Family. They are also hairy like most of this family. The leaves arise from an elongated, slender rhizome that creeps through the duff on the forest floor. The main tube of the flower is greenish-yellow or, sometimes, red-tinged. The petals are startling; they are finely divided and attract the attention of small insects as well as human passers-by. The common name for *mitella* is Mitrewort or Bishop's-cap, names inspired by its two-peaked seed capsule. The capsule originates from the fusing of two seed chambers (ovaries).

Naked Mitrewort is found in damp, mossy woods across the island of Newfoundland and north to northern Labrador. It is found in the boreal forest across North America, south to Montana in the west, and Pennsylvania in the east. It also grows in Asia.

Baie Verte

Crackerberry

Cornus canadensis L.
Dogwood Family
Cornaceae

In the sombre days of autumn, Crackerberries contrast sharply in colour with the wet greens and browns of the forest floor. *Cornus* is from *cornu*, a horn, and refers to the hardness of the wood of the shrubby members of the genus. *Canadensis* means Canadian.

Many of the Crackerberries in an area may be joined by an underground rhizome and, thus, are all the same plant. The flowering stems are about 10 to 20 centimetres tall and have one or two pairs of small leaves lower on the stem. There are generally two or three pairs of large leaves just below the flower, which appear to be in a whorl because of their attachment close together on the stem. Many flowers compose what appears to be one flower, resulting in a bunch of berries. The four white 'petals' are in fact bracts, leaves with a white pigment and often a rose tinge. The many small flowers are thus made noticeable, and pollination is easily effected as insects walk across the grouped flowers. Poinsettia uses a similar strategy. The fruit are drupes and have juicy but tasteless flesh. The single stone in each may be two-seeded but is often only one-seeded. The name Crackerberry comes from the sound made when the fruit is chewed. Each fruit is almost bursting with juice and a bite will release this pressure like the 'crack' of a whip.

This species grows all over Newfoundland and north to northern Labrador (Okak) in woods, bogs, heaths, headlands, and other habitats. It occurs from Greenland to Alaska and south to West Virginia in the east and California in the west. It also grows in northeastern Asia. A similar species is the smaller Swedish Bunchberry (*Cornus suecica* L.), which is restricted to cool sites near the coast. Its flowers are dark purple and its upper and lower leaves are similar in size and do not appear whorled.

Crackerberries can be munched while walking in the woods, but they are not usually a first choice for a snack. Laplanders boil Crackerberries in whey to make puddings, which are served with cream.

Baie Verte

Swedish Bunchberry

Cornus suecica L.
Dogwood Family
Cornaceae

This little gem, which is most often encountered on headlands, is a study in colour. The flowers are dark and the fruit are a deep red. *Cornus* is from the Latin *cornu*, horn, and refers to the hardness of the wood of shrubby species. *Suecica* means Swedish.

This species differs from Crackerberry (*Cornus canadensis* L.) in two main respects. The several pairs of leaves are scattered along the stem, whereas Crackerberry has a whorl at the top of the stem and a smaller pair farther down. The flowers, which are clustered in the centre of four white bracts, are dark purple, but greenish-white in Crackerberry. Bracts are coloured leaves that surround the flowers and attract pollinators. Bracts are also observed in poinsettias.

The Swedish Bunchberry grows on headland heaths throughout Newfoundland and Labrador. It grows on the coast of British Columbia, around Alaska, across northern Canada, and south to Nova Scotia. It also occurs in Greenland, Iceland, northern Europe, and northeastern Asia.

The fruit are juicier and tastier than those of Crackerberry. In Lapland, the fruit is mixed with whey, boiled until thick (seeds strained off), and the pudding served with cream.

Pacquet

Creeping Snowberry

Gaultheria hispidula (L.) Muhl.
Heath Family
Ericaceae

The Creeping Snowberry has various common names in Newfoundland and Labrador: Capillaire, Maidenhair, Magna-tea berry, Indian tea berry, and variations on these. *Gaultheria* commemorates Jean-François Gaulthier (1708-1756), a naturalist and court physician in Quebec, while *hispidula* means with sparse stiff hairs.

Extensive mats are often formed by the fine branching stems of the Creeping Snowberry. The evergreen leaves, which are retained on the plant for several years, are found towards the ends of the branches. The stems of this plant are often particularly elongated. Under certain environmental conditions, this dainty plant may be confused with Twinflower (*Linnaea borealis* L.) or Partridgeberry (*Vaccinium vitis-idaea* L.) when there are no flowers or fruit. It can always be distinguished, however, by the presence of short, stiff brown hairs on the lower leaf surface. Each of the minute flowers has two bracts at its base, four sepals, four petals, and eight stamens. The fruit, which resembles an ant's egg, is not a berry but a dry capsule containing numerous tiny seeds and enveloped by the calyx, which expands and becomes fleshy. Like the undersurface of the leaves, the calyx is covered with short, stiff brown hairs.

This species is found throughout the island of Newfoundland and north to central Labrador (Rigolet) in mossy woods. It also grows west to British Columbia and south to North Carolina.

The fruit has an exquisite flavour, like wintergreen but slightly more acidic, that is matched by few other fruit. The fruit is abundant in some patches, but picking it is usually a lengthy affair. The fruit should be preserved whole in syrup and enjoyed with cream. The leaves can be dried and used to make a tea on their own or mixed with other herbs.

Baie Verte

Starflower

Trientalis borealis Raf.
Primrose Family
Primulaceae

The name Starflower suits this plant, as it is an elaboration of starry patterns – the leaves, petals, and sepals. *Trientalis* is Latin for one-third of a foot and refers to the height of the plant. *Borealis* means northern.

This is a low perennial herb that arises from a slender rhizome and most, if not all, of the leaves are in a single whorl at the top of the stem. These plants are usually unbranched but there is a branched variety. The flower parts are generally in sevens but may vary from fives to nines. The sepals alternate with the petals, the bases of which are fused into a short tube. The stamens, which are attached to the base of the petal tube, have their bases connected into a ring. The seed capsule splits into five sections and contains a large number of seeds for its small size.

This species is found throughout Newfoundland and Labrador. It grows in woodlands, on peaty slopes, and even on hilltops in subalpine environments. It occurs west to Saskatchewan and south to West Virginia.

Baie Verte

145

One-flowered Wintergreen

Moneses uniflora (L.) Gray
Wintergreen Family
Pyrolaceae

This plant is found in the same habitats as the legendary trolls of Norse mythology and it has a quality about it that makes such a suggestion reasonable. *Moneses* is from the Greek, *monos*, meaning single and, *hesis*, meaning delight and refers to the single attractive flower on each plant. *Uniflora* means one-flowered.

One-flowered Wintergreen shoots, which arise from a slender creeping subterranean rhizome, have one to four sets of delicate leaves in twos opposite each other on the stem or in whorls of three. The single fragrant flower produced by each shoot is borne on a long stalk. It nods and has its parts in fives: five sepals, petals, and stigmas, but ten stamens. Some flowers may be found with the parts in fours. The petals are usually waxy-white but can be rose-tinged. The nodding habit of the flower helps to protect the pollen, which is easily spoiled by moisture, from being made wet by the dripping water and fog in the damp habitats where this plant grows. The seed capsule, however, is held erect, and, when it splits open, the seeds can be catapulted out by the wind. Late summer and autumn winds are gusty and jerk the capsule back and forth, throwing out the seeds.

The One-flowered Wintergreen is the only species in the genus. It is a circumboreal species found in damp woods and bogs. In Newfoundland, it is found in most parts of the island and north to northern Labrador (Nain); in North America, it occurs west to Alaska and south to West Virginia in the east and Colorado in the west. It also grows in Eurasia.

Baie Verte

Smaller Enchanter's Nightshade

Circaea alpina L.
Evening Primrose Family
Onagraceae

The Smaller Enchanter's Nightshade differs from other members of the family such as *Epilobium*, the willowherbs and fireweed, and *Oenothera*, the Evening Primrose. Dioscorides named this genus for *Circe*, the enchantress. *Alpina* means alpine.

This minute plant is easily overlooked on the forest floor. Its tiny flowers, pollinated by small flies, have two stamens that project outwards and a slightly longer style, with a knobby stigma between the stamens. Nectar is secreted in a ring around the base of the style. When a fly lands, it usually alights upon the style first, so the stigma receives pollen from the flower previously visited by the fly. As the insect forces its way to the nectar, it is dusted with pollen. Self-pollination is rare. Each fruit contains one seed and is covered with hooked hairs that aid in dispersal.

The Smaller Enchanter's Nightshade grows in moist woods here and there across the island of Newfoundland and north to central Labrador. It is also found west to the Aleutian Islands, south to California in the west and Georgia in the east, and in Eurasia.

Baie Verte

Indian Pipe

Monotropa uniflora L.
Wintergreen Family
Pyrolaceae

This ghostly flower is a pleasant surprise on a walk through a cool dark wooded area. *Monotropa* means one turn and refers to the nodding of the flower. *Uniflora* means one flower.

Indian Pipe lacks chlorophyll, the green pigment found in most plants. Although it cannot produce its own food, Indian Pipe gets nutrients through mycorrhiza, an association between a soil fungus and the roots of a plant where both the fungus and the plant benefit. The fungus, which forms a sheath around the root, digests rotting leaves and needles on the forest floor and provides nutrients, minerals, and water to the Indian Pipe. It is thought that Indian Pipe supplies the fungus with vitamins and other chemicals. The whole plant is usually white, but it may sometimes be tinged with pink.

The flower nods when it is open, but, as the fruit matures, the stem gradually straightens. By autumn the fruit capsule is upright atop the stem and the entire plant looks like a thin brown candlestick.

Indian Pipe is found throughout the island of Newfoundland and north to central Labrador (Goose Bay), particularly in woods that have a thick moist layer of needles and leaves. It grows throughout North America, south into Mexico, and also in Asia.

This plant turns black after it has been picked. After its seeds have been shed, it can be used in dried plant arrangements.

Baie Verte

Yellow Lady's-slipper

Cypripedium calceolus L.
Orchid Family
Orchidaceae

Orchids are considered exotic and rare by the general public and to botanists they represent a high level of advancement in structure and function. *Cypripedium* means slipper of Venus and *calceolus* means a small shoe.

The specimen in the illustration is unusually small for the species, but this is due to the harsh conditions under which it grew. Yellow Lady's-slipper usually ranges from 20 to 50 centimetres tall and has three to five leaves. There is one or, occasionally, two flowers on the end of each stem. The flower has the usual number of parts expected with a monocot, in threes or multiples of three. Its three sepals range in colour from yellowish-green with a brownish tinge to a bright claret in bog specimens. There are also three petals; the two lateral petals, which are the same colour as the sepals, are long, narrow, and twisted in the variety *pubescens*. In the variety *planipetalum*, the one in the illustration, the lateral petals are flat or twisted once. The third petal is the pouch; it is yellow with red spots on an in-turned margin. This entire beautiful flower is adapted to attract pollinators.

Cypripedium calceolus grows in Europe and Asia and is the only Lady's-slipper in Europe. There are two varieties of this species on the island of Newfoundland: variety *pubescens* (Willd.) Correll and variety *planipetalum* (Fern.) Vict. & Rousseau. Variety *pubescens* is found in the woods on the west coast, particularly in the Bonne Bay and Bay of Islands area. It extends south to Louisiana and west to southern Alaska. It also grows in certain localities in the mountains of the southwestern United States. Variety *planipetalum* (illustrated) grows on the treeless barrens of the Northern Peninsula amongst other dwarfed plants. It also grows along the northern shore of the St. Lawrence River as far as Ontario and on Anticosti Island.

Eddies Cove

153

Pink Lady's-slipper

Cypripedium acaule Ait.
Orchid Family
Orchidaceae

Pink Lady's-slipper grows amongst low shrubs around clearings in the woods. *Cypripedium* is from two Greek words – *Kypris*, who was Venus, the goddess of love and beauty, and *pedilon* meaning slipper. *Acaule* means stemless.

This species first grows singly, then later forms clumps. Each plant produces a pair of large light green leaves from the ground level, with no noticeable stems. The leaves are longitudinally ribbed and covered with hairs. The flowering stalk emerges from between the two leaves and bears a single flower which varies in colour. The sepals may range from yellow-green to greenish-brown, and the pouch is usually pink but may range from white to deep crimson. The opening to the pouch is different from that of any other Lady's-slipper in North America. It is similar, however, to *Cypripedium japonicum* of Japan. The opening is usually rounded, but in this species there is a cleft down the centre of the pouch, which has the margins folded in and many hairs. This slit is large enough to allow a fairly large bee to enter, sip the nectar, and effect pollination. In most orchids, the pollen of each anther is embedded in a mucilaginous substance to form a sticky mass that adheres to insect visitors. In a few orchids the pollen is dispersed in groups of four grains, but in this species, which is an exception, the pollen grains are dispersed singly.

Pink Lady's-slippers grow in the acidic soils of the woods of Newfoundland, except for the Northern Peninsula. They prefer dry sites and seem to grow mostly amongst the shrubbery around clearings in the woods. Some, however, grow in bogs and wet mossy sites. This species also ranges south to the mountains of northern Georgia and west through Manitoba to northern Alberta and into the Northwest Territories. There are two other Lady's-slippers in Newfoundland, one yellow and the other pink and white. When only leaves are present, this species can be confused with Clintonia, which has large leaves that look similar but are not as prominently ribbed and hairless as Clintonia.

This is a classic example of a wild flower that defies domestication. All plants that are transplanted from the woods disappear, so it should not be disturbed. It seems to grow in specific sites and cannot tolerate any environmental changes. An individual plant may or may not come up every year.

Barachois Pond Provincial Park

Common Strawberry

Fragaria virginiana Duchesne
Rose Family
Rosaceae

The word strawberry comes from the Anglo-Saxon *streawberige*. *Streaw* meant strew and straw is derived from it, since grass was strewn about to dry into hay and straw. The strawberry spreads by strewing its runners about, thus providing the derivation of the first part of its name. *Berige*, probably derived from a northern European language, means berry. *Fragaria* is from *fraga* and refers to the fragrance of the fruit. *Virginiana* means Virginian.

The short, stout stem rests at the soil surface and thrusts sturdy roots into the soil and firm leaves upwards. A variety described in Newfoundland and Labrador, *terrae-novae* (Rydb.) Fern. & Wieg., either has stiff hairs on the petioles and flower stalks or may be hairless. Runners arise from the bases of the leaves and are an effective means of spreading. They bear leaves at two points along the length: the first has a pair of tiny leaves, and the second produces a new plant which can, in turn, produce a runner. The flowers are typical of the Rose Family and are visited by bees and other pollinating insects. Some varieties of cultivated strawberry are self-sterile, so the fruit will not be produced unless there is another variety present to supply pollen. A strawberry is an example of a false fruit, since the luscious flesh is really only the end of the flower stalk that becomes enlarged and brightly coloured. The actual fruit are the little hard 'seeds' embedded in it.

The Common Strawberry grows in fields and along the edges of woods all over the island of Newfoundland and north to west-central Labrador. It also occurs west to Alberta and south to Oklahoma. The Woodland Strawberry, *Fragaria vesca* L., also grows on the island but less commonly. Its sepals spread away from the fruit even when it is young, and the 'seeds' are stuck on the surface, not sunken into pits, as in the Common Strawberry.

The leaves are dried to make herbal tea and the fruit is used in numerous ways.

Stephenville

Northern Comandra

Geocaulon lividum (Richards.) Fern.
Sandalwood Family
Santalaceae

It is a surprise to find Northern Comandra since it is uncommon; it usually grows as scattered sombre-looking individuals. *Geocaulon* is from the Greek *ge* meaning earth and *caulos* meaning stalk. It refers to the lower portion of the stem that extends below the soil surface for some distance before it reaches the rhizome. *Lividum* means lead-coloured.

This hairless plant arises from a subterranean brown or reddish rhizome. The unbranched stems are one to three centimetres tall and have lead-coloured or purplish leaves with untoothed margins. The flowers are borne in groups of three on a stalk. Only the central flower has both ovaries and stamens, while the others have only stamens. No petals are present, and in the bud the calyx lobes are joined along their edges to form a five-sided tent-like canopy over the developing flower parts. Since only one flower of a group has an ovary, only one fruit develops. The actual fruit is a nut, but it appears to be a berry since the calyx tube becomes fleshy and orange to scarlet-coloured.

The Northern Comandra grows in moss and damp humus in open woods or clearings in forests across Newfoundland and north to northern Labrador (Nain). It also occurs west to Alaska and south to northern New England, northern Minnesota, and southern British Columbia.

Baie Verte

Bearberry

Arctostaphylos uva-ursi (L.) Spreng.
Heath Family
Ericaceae

This plant is also known as Kinnikinick. It forms magnificent carpets on banks, at the edges of forests, and in other sunny locations. *Arctostaphylos* is loosely translated from the Greek *arctos*, bear, and *staphyle*, a bunch of grapes. *Uva-ursi* is the old genus name, which means bears' grape.

In certain habitats Bearberry grows beside Partridgeberry, but a closer look clearly distinguishes it. Bearberry's leaf is broader towards the tip than Partridgeberry, has a duller surface, and is fairly flat. The leaf of Partridgeberry has more parallel sides than Bearberry, a shiny surface, and is V-shaped in cross-section (there is a crease along the mid-vein). The flowers are clusters of hanging bells. The nectar is secreted at the base of the corolla, which is uppermost because the flowers hang down. A dense covering of hairs on the stamen filaments prevents the nectar from running down. The stamens are highly modified. The base of the stamen filament is narrow and tubular, and then swells out and is covered with hairs. It narrows again above the swell. The anthers have two lobes which have long, thin, thread-like appendages. Only skilled and determined bumblebees and honeybees reach the nectar, and pollen is transferred on their heads.

Bearberry, a circumboreal species, occurs across the island of Newfoundland and north to central Labrador. In North America it extends south to Newfoundland and Quebec, South Dakota, New Mexico, and Washington. Its range also includes Greenland, Iceland, and northern Eurasia.

While not flavourful, the fruit is reportedly palatable when cooked. Aboriginal Americans used the leaves to treat kidney and bladder infections.

Baie Verte

Blueberry

Vaccinium angustifolium Ait.
Heath Family
Ericaceae

Newfoundland and Labrador is blessed with an abundance of wild fruit, and the Blueberry is the chief amongst them. *Vaccinium*, an ancient name for this fruit, is presumably from the Latin *vaccinus*, meaning cows. *Angustifolium* means narrow-leafed.

The height of this shrub can vary considerably (5 to 25 centimetres), but the best-producing plants are about 15 to 20 centimetres high. They form clumps and spread by underground stems. The young branchlets are green, while the older stems develop a reddish-brown bark. During the winter the twigs bear two types of buds: smaller ones that produce new shoots, and larger swollen ones at the ends of the branches that produce flowers. The leaves have a shiny, bright green upper surface and a paler lower surface. The margins have many small teeth, each of which is tipped with a bristle. In autumn, the leaves are scarlet and set the hillsides and barrens ablaze with colour.

Blueberry flowers are not conspicuous and have no perfume, but bees and other insects eagerly seek their abundant nectar. The five petals are fused, except at their tips, to form an urn-shaped corolla. The style and stigma protrude from the corolla and the stamens are grouped around the style. When a bee visits a flower, it must extend its tongue to the nectar at the base of the style. As it probes, it disturbs the anthers, and pollen falls onto its head. When it visits another flower, it touches the stigma with its head and effects cross-pollination. The fruit are blue with a whitish bloom that consists of small flakes of wax. One variety, which has black fruit and lacks the characteristic waxy bloom, is found occasionally. Blueberries contain numerous small seeds.

This species is the common Blueberry found all over the island of Newfoundland and north to northern Labrador, except in wet habitats. It grows throughout much of eastern North America. It might be confused with one of the two Huckleberries (*Gaylussacia*) native to the island. Huckleberries can be distinguished by their 10 hard seeds in each fruit and leaves covered with small dots of resin.

Blueberries are eaten by humans, birds, and several mammal species. During the winter, the flower buds are relished by ptarmigans and hares. The berries are used for jam, jelly, pies, muffins, wine, grunts, and other sweets. They can be dried and used like currants. Blueberries help control blood sugar levels in diabetics.

Baie Verte

Raspberry

Rubus idaeus L.
Rose Family
Rosaceae

The luscious fruit of this plant has been enjoyed by most, grown by many, and celebrated in prose and verse by some throughout the centuries. *Rubus* is the Roman name for the raspberry and it is derived from *ruber*, meaning red. *Idaeus* means of Mt. Ida.

Raspberry stems are called canes and the briefest acquaintance with them confirms that they are covered with prickles. These prickles are stiff, woody hairs intended to protect the plant from browsing animals. The canes are sent up from underground stems and bear many leaves that are whitened beneath. During their second year each cane produces flowers, then fruit. The five sepals, which are fused to each other, the five petals, and the numerous stamens seen in raspberry flowers are characteristic of the entire Rose Family. The Raspberry is an 'aggregate fruit.' As each individual fruit ripens, it enlarges, and all of the adjacent fruit become crowded into a coherent thimble-like structure.

There is only one Raspberry in Newfoundland, but the fruit of other *Rubus* species – blackberries, plumboys, and bakeapples – are similar. *Rubus idaeus* was introduced from Europe and has become thoroughly naturalized. Its seeds are dispersed by birds and other animals, and plants spring up in clearings, burnt-over areas, and roadsides. This species is found throughout the Northern Hemisphere.

Raspberries are used to make jam, jelly, pies, wine, and other treats. The leaves are used with other herbs to make tea.

Baie Verte

Fireweed

Epilobium angustifolium L.
Evening Primrose Family
Onagraceae

Fireweed is one of the first plants to grow in an area ravaged by fire and, when in bloom, its beauty 'heals' the scar. *Epilobium* means upon a capsule and refers to the inferior ovary. *Angustifolium* means narrow-leafed.

The stem is usually about one metre in height but it can rise much higher. The roots in the extensive root system have the unusual ability to form buds that grow into new plants. In this way a single plant soon forms a large clump. After a fire, when the above-ground portions are gone, new stems arise from their roots. The flowers range in colour from magenta to pure white, with intermediate forms that have white petals and pink sepals. The flower goes through several phases, all of which are directed towards cross-pollination. Nectar is secreted by the top of the ovary. Since this flower has an inferior ovary, the sepals, petals, and stamens are attached to the top of the ovary. The bases of the filaments form a hollow cone around the style over the nectar, and there are hairs on the style just above this cone. These two structures protect the nectar from rain but allow insects to reach it with their tongues. When the flower first opens, the style is short and the stamens bent outwards so that insects can land on them. The anthers are covered with pollen grains bound together by sticky threads that help attach them to the feet of insects. The stamens later bend inwards, and the style elongates as the four large divergent stigmas expand. The stigmas then form the only landing site for any visiting insects. In this way insects pollinate older flowers with pollen from younger flowers. If pollination is not effected by insects, then the stigmas curl downwards and touch the anthers, making self-pollination possible. When the capsule is mature and splits open, the seeds are borne on the wind with the aid of a tuft of fine hair on each seed.

This species occurs throughout Newfoundland and Labrador. It is one of the first plants to colonize cleared areas, burnt-over woods, and roadsides. It is circumpolar in distribution and occurs in most of North America, except for the southern parts and the Great Plains.

The young shoots of Fireweed can be used as greens; however, boiling in two waters may be necessary to remove its bitter taste. The leaves can be dried and used in herbal tea mixtures and the Aboriginals of northwestern North America are reported to have used the pith of the stems to make a thick soup.

Baie Verte

Flat-topped White Aster

Aster umbellatus Mill.
Daisy Family
Compositae

Non-conformists are often difficult to accept within a society but yet are a part of it, and so it is with asters. Most have mauve or blue flowers and, when a white-flowered species is encountered, it receives a second glance. *Aster*, from the Greek *aster*, means star, which refers to the appearance of the flower. *Umbellatus* means umbellate and refers to the flat-topped inflorescence.

These are stiff, neat-looking plants with smooth reddish stems and smooth-edged, gracefully tapering leaves. Solitary stems arise from coarse, creeping rhizomes and have leaves along their entire length. They generally reach a height of over one metre. The lowest branches of the inflorescence are the longest and gradually become shorter towards the tip. This arrangement brings the flowers into a plane and serves a significant function in pollination. The flowers become noticeable in a large grouping, and pollinating insects can easily crawl from one to another.

A considerable variation in this species can cause confusion. The above description and the illustration fit the typically encountered specimen, but plants vary in height from 25 centimetres to two metres. The leaves may be hairy on the lower surface and their margins may be distinctly toothed. They are all in the same species, however, and such variation can occur because the essential features that separate this group of plants are still present.

The Flat-topped White Aster grows in thickets and open woods across the island of Newfoundland except on the Northern Peninsula. Its range extends west to Minnesota and south to Georgia.

Baie Verte

169

Balsam Ragwort

Senecio pauperculus Michx.
Daisy Family
Compositae

The original meaning of Ragwort has been lost with time; however, wort is the Anglo-Saxon word for plant or herb, and rag could refer to the ragged appearance of the leaves. *Senecio*, from *senex* which means old man, refers to the hoary appearance which results from a white cobweb of hairs all over the plant. *Pauperculus* means poor.

This plant is 'poor' in its overall aspect because it has few leaves and flowers. The basal leaves and flowering stem of this perennial arise from a slender often-branching rhizome. The stem may grow to 30 centimetres in height, but it is often shorter in a harsh environment. There may be just a tuft of basal leaves when a plant does not flower, or the basal leaves may be found at the base of the flowering stem (as shown in the illustration). The stem is usually hairless; although there may be scattered tufts of white woolly hair, these are insufficient in quantity to make the plant appear hoary. The leaf shape varies considerably from plant to plant and from base to top of one plant. There may only be a few flowers, but some plants have as many as 30. Seed dispersal is achieved by several mechanisms. Each seed of *Senecio* has a tuft of hairs (pappus) on the end that acts as a parachute. A further mechanism ensures that the seeds get firmly anchored to the ground. Seed glands exude a sticky slime, and after the seed is attached to the ground, the pappus blows away and a new generation commences.

Senecio, with 2,500 species, is the largest genus in the Daisy Family. The cosmopolitan Balsam Ragwort grows in gravelly areas, bogs, and hilltops all across Newfoundland, north to western Labrador (Carol Lake), west to Alaska, and south to higher areas in Virginia in the east and British Columbia in the west. There are 11 species in Newfoundland and seven in Labrador.

Lomond

Island Gentian

Gentianella detonsa (Rottb.) G. Don ssp. *nesophila* (T. Holm) Gillett
Gentian Family
Gentianaceae

The tourist industry has popularized the dark blue trumpet-shaped gentians of Switzerland. Newfoundland and Labrador has similar gentians. Its Latin name is rather complicated because of recent taxonomic revisions. *Gentianella* means little gentian and *Gentiana* is from Gentius, ancient king of Illyria, who discovered the medicinal virtue of the plant. *Detonsa* means shaved downwards and *nesophila* means island-loving.

These plants are biennials, although some individuals may only be annuals. The opposite, slightly fleshy whitened leaves are found on the flowering stalks. The flowers are borne singly on the ends of stems and have four calyx lobes, four corolla lobes, and four stamens. The stamen filaments are fused to the corolla tube at their bases. The colour may vary from dark to light blue, and the mature seed capsule, which is as long as the corolla, contains numerous seeds. Gentians are highly prized by gardeners who specialize in rock garden and alpine plants. These plants are not cooperative; the seeds are extremely difficult to germinate, but good results have been obtained by planting them outside in the autumn. They then germinate in the spring after remaining dormant in the frozen soil during the winter months.

This species is circumpolar in distribution. In North America it occurs across the arctic and southward on the east to Quebec and Newfoundland and Labrador, and on the west through Alaska and the Rocky Mountains to the Sierra Madre of Mexico. The subspecies *nesophila* grows in rocky calcareous soils all along the western coast of Newfoundland, on the Mingan Islands, Anticosti, and the east coast of James Bay. Of the five species of gentians in Newfoundland and Labrador, one lives only on the island of Newfoundland, two solely in Labrador, and two in both parts of the province. The Island Gentian is the only one with a single flower on each stem.

Daniel's Harbour

173

Yellow Mountain Saxifrage

Saxifraga aizoides L.
Saxifrage Family
Saxifragaceae

Saxifrages need to be viewed at close range in order to appreciate the intricate patterns on their petals. *Saxifraga*, meaning to break a stone, is derived from the use of certain European species during medieval times to dissolve kidney stones. *Aizoides* means similar to *Aizoon* (an African shrub).

The Yellow Mountain Saxifrage is a fleshy plant with plump, pointed leaves. It forms a neat clump until it starts to flower, and then it becomes a sprawling mass of dainty yellow flowers. These are characterized by having the nectar fully exposed, by being yellow-coloured with spots, and by emitting a nauseous odour suggestive of decaying meat. These combined features attract small flies, bees, small butterflies, ants, and small beetles. In these flowers the petals open out flat to expose the stamens and ovary, which has two styles with small stigmas on their tips. Nectar is secreted around the base of the ovary. The flowers are specialized to ensure cross-pollination. The stamens release their pollen one anther after another, starting with the outer ones, until all ten have opened. Only then do the stigmas become sticky and receive pollen. In this way, pollen must come from another plant.

This species occurs on the west coast and less frequently on the south coast of Newfoundland, and north to northern Labrador. It particularly likes calcareous gravels or cool and damp slopes. It occurs in the arctic regions of North America and Eurasia. In North America it extends south in suitable locations to the Gaspe, Vermont, New York, Alberta, and British Columbia.

Portland Creek

Smoothleaf Mountain Avens

Dryas integrifolia Vahl
Rose Family
Rosaceae

This plant produces a lovely flower in a severe habitat. *Dryas* is named for the Dryads, or wood nymphs, and *integrifolia* means untoothed leaves.

This plant commonly forms a mat of woody stems hidden beneath its evergreen leaves. The leaves are broadest at the base where they may have one or two teeth. The edge of the leaf is rolled under except at the base. The upper surface is a dark shiny green, but one form has a covering of dense hairs. The under surface has a dense covering of white hairs. The leaves remain on the plant for a year or two after they die, then they gradually add to the humus that accumulates under the stems.

The singly borne, erect flowers have eight to 10 petals and numerous stamens. Each fruit retains the style, which becomes elongated and feathery. The styles are smoky-white or tinged with brown and tend to twist together until the fruit are ready to be dispersed. Each hair along the style has a structure at its base, which allows it to respond to moisture. When wet they clasp the style and when dry they spread out. This ensures that the fruit will be most likely to float on the wind on a dry day when they have a better chance of being carried for some distance.

This species grow on calcareous barrens and cliffs or talus slopes of western Newfoundland from Port-aux-Basques to the tip of the Northern Peninsula and throughout Labrador.

St. Anthony

Small-flowered Grass-of-Parnassus

Parnassia parviflora DC
Saxifrage Family
Saxifragaceae

This and other Grasses-of-Parnassus are arctic plants that only occur farther south in cool habitats. *Parnassia* is named for Mount Parnassus and *parviflora* means small-flowered. The Grass-of-Parnassus mentioned by the first-century Greek physician Dioscorides is thought to be *Parnassia palustris*, which also occurs in the province.

The fleshy leaves are in a basal rosette. The flowering stalk arises from the rosette and bears a single leaf and flower. There are five normal stamens in an outer whorl, which alternate with five staminodes in an inner whorl. The stamens curve in over the ovary. The staminodes are attached to the petals by their bases. They have a solid base that secretes nectar, and a fan-shaped group of five to seven filaments of unequal length. Each filament ends in a glistening yellow knob, which looks like a nectary. The appearance of nectar attracts small flies. They find nectar at the base of the staminodes and effect pollination in their efforts to sip it. This flower exudes perfume, but only during the day when pollinating insects are active.

The Small-flowered Grass-of-Parnassus is fairly common on the west coast and Northern Peninsula of the island of Newfoundland and in Labrador, where they grow on wet calcareous soils. This species is found as far west as Alaska and south to Michigan and Utah. Four species grow on the island of Newfoundland, all of which occur mainly on the west coast and Northern Peninsula. Three of the species also occur in Labrador. The plants differ from each other in leaf shape and some aspects of their petals and staminodes.

River of Ponds Park

Purple Mountain Saxifrage

Saxifraga oppositifolia L.
Saxifrage Family
Saxifragaceae

Purple Mountain Saxifrage flowers are such an intensely dark burgundy colour that on a dull day they are not easily seen. *Saxifraga*, from *saxum*, stone, and *frangere*, to break, refers to the use of some species to treat kidney stones. *Oppositifolia* means opposite leaves.

This is a compact, mat-forming species. The leaves are plump wedges attached in an opposite fashion, with a fringe of hairs along the margins. Plants that grow in harsh environments often have alternate strategies to ensure pollination and seed-set. In cold northern climates, the scarcity of insects causes these species to self-pollinate. Cross-pollination is, however, favoured. Saxifrages have exposed nectar and are usually pollinated by flies, which are attracted by their nauseous flowers. Their 'perfume' smells like rotting meat or feces, both good places for flies to lay eggs.

This species grows in calcareous substrates in western Newfoundland, the Northern Peninsula, and coastal Labrador. In North America it grows around the Gulf of St. Lawrence, northern New England, James Bay, and the mountains of the northwestern United States. It is also found in Eurasia.

Cape St. George

Hyssop-leafed Fleabane

Erigeron hyssopifolius Michx.
Daisy Family
Compositae

Members of this genus have been used to repel fleas but, unfortunately, there is no record of this particular plant accomplishing that purpose. *Erigeron*, from the Greek *eri* meaning early and *geron* meaning old man, was the ancient name of a plant that bloomed early and was covered with long white hairs. *Hyssopifolius* means hyssop-leafed. The Hyssop is a European herb used in cooking and in the liqueur, Chartreuse.

Hyssop-leafed Fleabane forms dense clumps up to 20 centimetres high. The margins of the narrow leaves curl under and have stiff hairs; hairs are also scattered on the surfaces of the leaves. The stem is densely covered with short, stiff hairs. The dainty flowers arise on the more-or-less leafless stalks above the clump. This plant, like other members of the Compositae, does not bear flowers singly. The flowers, called florets, are grouped together into an inflorescence called a capitulum and are surrounded by phyllaries, green bracts. Capitula have two types of florets: disc and ray florets. The disc florets of this plant, found in the centre of the capitulum, are yellow and have a tubular corolla, with five equal points. The ray florets have a mauve corolla, which has an elongated portion called a ligule. The ligule is what is plucked from the Ox-eye Daisy to determine whether love is reciprocated. The calyx of the florets may be modified into plumed hairs which act as parachutes for dispersing the seeds on the wind. The capitulum is one strategy that plants use to attract insects. Each floret is small and would remain unnoticed; however, when the florets are grouped and have a yellow landing pad with mauve runways converging on it, it attracts insects. Nectar and pollen are provided in most Composites.

Hyssop-leafed Fleabane grows on rocky, calcareous soils in western Newfoundland and on scattered sites in the central part of the island. This species occurs from Newfoundland to the Yukon and south to New England and Michigan. There are eight species of *Erigeron* on the island, but the others do not usually have the characteristic dense clumps of short stems with narrow leaves.

Gros Morne National Park

Aizoon Saxifrage

Saxifraga aizoon Jacq.
Saxifrage Family
Saxifragaceae

Aizoon Saxifrage is an arctic plant that descends southwards to favoured spots on the continents of the Northern Hemisphere. *Saxifraga,*which means to break a stone, originates in the old doctrine of signatures employed by early European herbalists: if a plant resembled a human organ or disease condition, it could be used to treat it. As a consequence, plants were named lungworts, spleenworts, and liverworts; wort is an Anglo-Saxon word meaning herb. Some European species bear granular bulblets which resemble kidney stones and were believed to dissolve them. The species name, *aizoon*, resulted from the plant's resemblance to the African succulent, *Aizoon*.

This species is easily recognized from even a single leaf of the rosette, since the leaves have chalk glands along the margins at their base of each tooth that secrete lime in the form of calcium bicarbonate. The lime is seen as solid calcareous deposits, and the quantity secreted is governed by the amount of calcium in the soil. The plant is presumably forced to take up excess calcium with other nutrients from the soil and this excess is secreted. The flowering stem can range in height from five to 30 centimetres. The petals are usually red-dotted. The perfume of this flower, although rather unpleasant, effectively attracts small flies that cross-pollinate the plants. The two-horned seed capsule is enclosed by the calyx at its base and is about one-half centimetre long.

The Aizoon Saxifrage is found in calcareous regions of the west coast of Newfoundland, the Northern Peninsula, and north to northern Labrador. It also occurs in scattered sites along Notre Dame Bay and as far east as Gambo. This species is circumpolar in distribution. In North America it extends south to mountain peaks in New England, northern Michigan and Minnesota, and Saskatchewan. It is the only species in the province that has lime deposits on its leaves.

Some larger forms of this species are cultivated in gardens and make attractive rock garden specimens.

Bellevue Beach Provincial Park

185

St. Lawrence Bird's-eye Primrose

Primula laurentiana Fern.
Primrose Family
Primulaceae

This plant is dainty perfection. There are numerous primroses in gardens around the world but only a few North American Bird's-eye Primroses in specialist's collections. *Primula* is from *primus*, early spring, the season when many primroses bloom. *Laurentiana* means of the St. Lawrence River.

The rosettes of leaves are nestled in the grass on headlands and heaths. The naked (i.e., leafless) scape rises and supports a cluster of flowers. The height of the scape varies with the amount of wind. These plants are farinose (they appear to be dusted with flour). This mealy coating consists of slender needles of a resinous or fatty substance secreted by short glandular hairs, which may deter insect pests. The flowers have a long slender floral tube that allows only long-tongued insects, like butterflies, to reach the nectar. The stamens are epipetalous, that is they are attached to the base of the floral tube (i.e., corolla).

This species grows on calcareous cliffs and meadows of western and northern Newfoundland and north to central Labrador. It is also found from eastern Quebec to Nova Scotia and northern Maine.

Port au Port Peninsula

Many-rayed Goldenrod

Solidago multiradiata Ait.
Daisy Family
Compositae

Banks of goldenrod line roadsides and fields, but this species is found in more rugged habitats. *Solidago*, from *soldus* meaning whole, probably refers to its past use in treating wounds. *Multiradiata* means many-rayed.

The basal leaves clustered at the base of the stem are glabrous (hairless) and oblanceolate (broader towards the tip). The leaves on the stem are broadest at the midpoint of the leaf. This is one of several arrangements of leaves found in goldenrods. The 'flowers' are large compared with other goldenrods such as the Rough-stemmed Goldenrod.. Each 'flower' has about 30 to 45 florets, with 12 to 20 of them ray florets. A capitulum ('flower') is a whole inflorescence compressed into a small packet. Each floret is a whole flower and it is grouped and surrounded by bracts, which are small leaf-like structures found at the base of flowers in an inflorescence. The bracts, called phyllaries, are collectively known as an involucre. In an Ox-eye Daisy, the disc florets are the regular-shaped yellow ones in the centre, and the ray florets ring the outside and have white strap-like extensions.

This species is found across Newfoundland and Labrador on peaty or calcareous soils. It is also found across the boreal and subarctic regions of North America and into Siberia.

Twillingate

St. John Oxytropis

Oxytropis johannensis Fern.
Pea Family
Leguminosae

Many members of the Pea Family have charming flowers of intricate structure and bright, clear colours. *Oxytropis* is from the Greek *oxys* meaning sharp and *tropis* meaning keel and refers to the keel of the flower. *Johannensis* means of the St. John River, which flows through New Brunswick and Maine.

Several leaves terminate each tough, stout stem. The stems are all connected to a strong taproot. Since these plants grow in arctic-alpine situations where the surface layer of soil is usually churned by frost, the plant must be securely rooted. The dissected nature and clump arrangement of the leaves are also important adaptations to a windy environment. The flowers are typical Pea Family flowers: an erect standard and a purple-veined white centre. The keel, which consists of two petals enveloping the pistil and stamens, has two wings on either side. The fruit is like a long narrow pea pod and is protected during its development by the tough calyx.

St. John Oxytropis grows on calcareous sites along the west coast, Northern Peninsula, Baie Verte Peninsula, and north to south-central Labrador. It also occurs west to James Bay and south to the St. John River. The two genera, *Oxytropis* and *Astragalus*, form a large and varied group.

Pacquet

Moss Campion

Silene acaulis L.
Pink Family
Caryophyllaceae

Moss Campion is an arctic-alpine plant that finds some of Newfoundland and Labrador's hilltops and coastal cliffs to its liking. *Silene* is from Silenus, the foster-father of Bacchus, god of wine. Some species of *Silene* have sticky substances on their stems. *Acaulis* means stemless and refers to growth habit.

This plant has two main forms in Newfoundland and Labrador: either sprawling or domed. The domed or igloo form is well adapted to windswept sites, as it resists wind damage and is a heat trap which enables the plants to grow and flower in cool habitats. A related, sprawling variety of this plant grows in less windy locations. The small narrow leaves of both forms have fine hairs along their margins.

The attractive flowers are either pink or, more rarely, white in Newfoundland and Labrador. They are raised just above the surface of the plant – pink Maiden Pink-like flowers on a grass-like carpet. Each plant may flower several times in one summer.

Moss Campion is mainly found in coastal sites and is particularly abundant on the west coast of the island of Newfoundland, the Northern Peninsula, and throughout Labrador. It grows in soil rich in calcium, either naturally occurring or added by seabird droppings and shells. This species also grows in several places in Nova Scotia, New Hampshire, and Quebec, and in mountainous areas of western North America and Eurasia.

This species is not present in large numbers in Newfoundland and Labrador. In Iceland, where it is abundant, it is boiled and eaten with butter.

Bottle Cove

Sea Thrift

Armeria maritima (Mill.) Willd.
Leadwort Family
Plumbaginaceae

Flower lollipops in tufts of grass are obviously a trick of the trolls to lure unsuspecting people into rocky barrens. *Armeria* is thought to be of Celtic origin and *maritima* means of seashores.

The illustration shows several flowering and fruiting portions separated from dense clumps. One large taproot anchors each clump, which consists of densely packed tufts of leaves. The narrow leaves are greyish-green and vary from three to eight centimetres in length. The flowering stalks need to be structurally strong to withstand fierce winds, and they accomplish that by being hollow. The flowers are borne in a cup of broad, brown bracts. The sepals form a whitish papery cone (right flower head in illustration), and, when the seeds are mature, this acts as a parachute for wind dispersal. This species has different types of flowers, as does Purple Loosestrife. There are two varieties of Sea Thrift: Type A has almost smooth stigmas and large, rough-coated pollen grains, while Type B has rough stigmas and small, smooth-coated pollen grains. The style is the same length in both types. The two types must be cross-pollinated; Type A pollen will only germinate on Type B stigmas, and vice versa.

Sea Thrifts are found on calcareous barrens and serpentine areas from Bay St. George to the Straits of Belle Isle on the island of Newfoundland and also in Labrador. The mostly northern species is circumboreal in its distribution.

This plant is used in Iceland as greens: cleaned of soil and dead leaves, it is boiled in milk, and served with butter. Selected cultivars are available in garden centres.

Trout River

Three-toothed Cinquefoil

Potentilla tridentata Ait.
Rose Family
Rosaceae

This is a common plant in many parts of Newfoundland and Labrador, but it should not be overlooked because of its abundance. There is much beauty in its dainty flowers and an elegance about its glossy leaves. *Potentilla* is from *potens* which means powerful and refers to the medicinal qualities thought to be in *Potentilla anserina*. *Tridentata* means three-toothed.

Each clump has a system of stout, branching stems just below the soil surface; the stems are woody and have a flaking bark. The flowering stalks rise and branch considerably. A simplified leaf is found at each point of branching. The leaves are lustrous green above and paler beneath. Each of the three leaflets has three teeth at its tip, while larger leaves may have five teeth. The calyx is different from most in that it has a calyculus. The Strawberry, this species, and others in the Rose Family have this structure. The saucer-shaped calyx has an inner whorl of five broad segments that are the free tips of the sepals, since a calyx consists of a whorl of sepals that have their bases fused. The calyculus is the outer ring of five smaller segments that alternate with the sepal tips. Most specimens have snowy-white petals; however, *aurora* ('like the dawn') has pink petals. Hairy seeds formed in each flower are dispersed by the wind.

When visiting the west coast of the island, the Northern Peninsula, or Labrador, check the Three-toothed Cinquefoils for those with hairy leaves. They could be Sibbaldia (*Sibbaldia procumbens* L.), an arctic species that extends to a few southern locations. Three-toothed Cinquefoil grows in dry, open sites such as hilltops, roadsides, rock crevices, and heaths of Newfoundland and Labrador. It occurs west to the Yukon and south on exposed mountains to Georgia.

St. John's

Partridgeberry/Redberry

Vaccinium vitis-idaea L.
Heath Family
Ericaceae

A handful of Partridgeberries makes a walk on headlands and heaths in the autumn a real pleasure. Partridgeberries are especially delicious, although more fragile for picking, after a frost. *Vaccinium*, an ancient name for these plants, may be derived from the Latin *vaccinus*, which means cows. *Vitis-idaea* means grape of Mt. Ida, the highest summit on Crete.

This evergreen shrub forms mats on the ground in open habitats or very short tufts in the shade of trees or shrubs. The oval leaves are a glossy dark green above and paler below. The centre of the leaf is furrowed and, thus, V-shaped in cross-section. The flowers are pinkish and resemble blueberry blossoms. On rocky barren hills where the soil is usually dry and the winds are drying, these plants are especially adapted to take advantage of any moisture, even fog. Small club-shaped hairs sunk in the leaf surface quickly absorb any water and transfer it to the tissues that carry on photosynthesis. Many of these dwarf plants which grow in exposed environments are long lived; Partridgeberries reportedly do not start to flower until they are 14 to 20 years of age. The dark red berries ripen by late September or early October. Fruit found clinging to the plants in the spring remain tasty.

Partridgeberries grow on heaths, barrens, woods, and headlands throughout Newfoundland and Labrador. They are circumpolar in distribution. In North America they are found in the Maritimes, the northern part of the rest of Canada, and Alaska. Partridgeberry plants can be confused with Creeping Snowberry (*Gaultheria hispidula* (L.) Bigel) and Bearberry (*Arctostaphylos uva-ursi* (L.) Spreng.) in woods and other habitats. The Creeping Snowberry has an almost flat leaf, pointed at both ends, with brown hairs underneath, and white spindle-shaped fruit with brown hairs. Bearberry leaves are broader near the tip and distinctly narrowed to the base, and have dull, dark red fruit with a pulpy white flesh.

Partridgeberries are used in pies, tarts, and jam. Traditionally, the fruit was stored in barrels of water. Birds and animals feast on the berries in the autumn and winter.

Baie Verte

Sheep Laurel

Kalmia angustifolia L.
Heath Family
Ericaceae

Sheep Laurel with its clusters of pink saucers is a beautiful but deadly plant. *Kalmia* commemorates Pehr Kalm (1716-1779), a student of Linnaeus, who collected plants in North America. *Angustifolia* means narrow-leafed.

This shrub forms large clumps by means of subterranean rhizomes and may grow to a height of one metre. The leathery, dark green evergreen leaves occur in whorls of three on the stem. They remain on the plant for about one and one-half years. The purplish-mauve spotting on many leaves is caused by rust, a fungal parasite. The new growth is well developed when the flowers open and a mass of blooms is found below a tuft of leaves. In addition to the usual pink, a white-flowered form grows in Newfoundland, but it is rare. The saucer-shaped corolla has 10 pockets that hold the anthers. If an insect lands on the flower, the anthers are released, and, functioning like a catapult, they shower the insect with pollen. Most pollen is produced in tetrads but released as separate grains; however, in the Heath Family, the pollen is produced and released in tetrads. A tetrad has three spherical pollen grains forming a triangular base with a fourth placed on top to give a pyramid-like shape.

This species is found on bogs, heaths, and forested areas across Newfoundland and north to central Labrador (Goose Bay). Its range extends west to Manitoba and south to the mountains of Georgia. It covers large areas of the island and is a problem to the forest industry. It quickly establishes itself after a forest has been decimated by fire or cutting and then interferes with the re-establishment of the forest by chemical warfare, secreting a substance which inhibits the growth of spruce seedlings. Another species, the Bog Laurel (*Kalmia polifolia* Wang.), grows in bogs and other wet habitats, and has opposite leaves and flowers borne on the ends of its branches.

Sheep Laurel is also appropriately called Lambkill. Since this plant is evergreen, it is present in the spring when sheep, goats, cattle, and horses are released from barns. These animals crave green plants and eat plants they would not normally touch, including Sheep Laurel. This plant contains the poison andromedotoxin; injesting even a small amount of the plant may result in severe illness or death.

Beothuk Park

New York Aster

Aster novi-belgii L.
Daisy Family
Compositae

The colour of these flowers, when viewed in the crisp and clear light of early September on a grassy bank above the sea, is inspiring. *Aster*, Greek for star, refers to the starry appearance of the flower. In early herbals these plants were called starworts. *Novi-belgii* means of New Belgium, an early name for New York.

The height and leaves of this plant vary. Its stems rise from a creeping rhizome and may vary in height from 20 centimetres near the sea to one metre in a sheltered location. The leaf bases clasp the stem with small lobes, and the margins are smooth (as illustrated) or irregularly toothed. The leaves are shiny green and often fleshy. The 'flowers' are inflorescences typical of this family. The yellow florets in the centre and the outer ring of florets with mauve strap-like extensions of the corolla are held in a 'vase' (involucre) consisting of minute leaf-like structures (phyllaries). These do not spread as much in some plants as that shown in the illustration. The florets with the mauve rays have only female parts, while the central yellow florets have both sexes. After the floret opens, the style grows longer, and, as it grows, its hairs sweep pollen from adjacent anthers. Bees, flies, butterflies, and other insects that visit the 'flower' are dusted with pollen, and, when they visit other 'flowers' with expanded and sticky stigmas, pollination occurs.

New York Asters grow across the island of Newfoundland and north to southern Labrador, with a population in central Labrador. There are 11 Aster species on the island, four in Labrador. They also occur south to Georgia, mostly within 60 kilometres of the sea.

Asters are not used medicinally in the twenty-first century, but Pliny suggested stewed Asters for snake bites and an amulet of Asters for sciatica. Virgil prescribed Aster root as a physic for ailing bees and the Shakers used a concoction of Asters to clear up skin disorders.

Baie Verte

202

Scotch Lovage

Ligusticum scothicum L.
Parsley Family
Umbelliferae

This plant, also known as Alexanders in certain parts of Newfoundland and Labrador, stands out boldly among the fine blades of grass that usually grow around it. *Ligusticum* means from the Liguria, a region of northwestern Italy where the garden herb, lovage, grows in abundance. *Scothicum* means Scotch.

The large basal leaves and stems spring from aromatic roots. The entire plant is hairless and, on older portions of the plant, the stems are reddish and ribbed. The leaves, which are compound and have leaflets in threes, have sheathing bases. The family, Umbelliferae, has an inflorescence, the umbel, which characterizes the family. Scotch Lovage has a compound umbel. The main branches of the inflorescence arise from a point and they in turn have a cluster of branches on their tips. This results in a flat-topped cluster of flowers, which are convenient for insects to investigate and effect pollination. The fruit are ribbed and at maturity they split into two. They often contain aromatic oils, as do caraway, anise, and fennel.

Scotch Lovage is found in salt marshes and on cliffs by the sea all around the coast of Newfoundland and Labrador. It occurs from Greenland to New York on this side of the Atlantic. It is also native in northern Europe.

The leaves have a strong parsley flavour and are used in salads, soups, stews, and the young stems can be candied and used like angelica.

Fischell

Harebell

Campanula rotundifolia L.
Bluebell Family
Campanulaceae

The Harebell looks fragile and delicate but it is well adapted to its environment. It thrusts its bells into the air from hollows on wind-swept headlands. *Campanula* means little bell and *rotundifolia* means round-leafed.

The species name, *rotundifolia*, may puzzle some because Harebells usually have long, narrow leaves. The Harebell, however, has both juvenile and mature leaves. The juvenile leaves occur close to the ground and are basically round in outline (see illustration), while the mature leaves, which come off the stem, are long and narrow. The juvenile leaves have usually withered by the time the plant flowers, but some young plants may be found in the vicinity of a flowering plant. The corolla may be blue, or, rarely, white or pink. The stamens help protect the nectar. The base of each filament is expanded and fused to the adjacent one. These bend in towards the style to form a dome over the nectar, to protect the nectar from being robbed by insects that are too small to effect pollination. The seed capsules are intricate, and often only a skeleton remains after a winter, which is attractive in flower arrangements.

Harebells grow all over Newfoundland and Labrador in meadows and on open rocky banks, and are particularly common on headlands and small islands. They grow throughout North America, but are mostly confined to higher altitudes in the south.

Trout River

206

Yellow Rattle

Rhinanthus crista-galli L.
Figwort Family
Scrophulariaceae

Yellow Rattle is often noticed after brushing past it in the grass on a headland because it does rattle. Seeds bang about in their seed capsules and make a noise. *Rhinanthus* is from the Greek meaning snout flower, although the plant that inspired this name is now classified in a different genus. *Crista-galli* means cock's comb.

The stems branch and rise to about 50 centimetres. *Rhinanthus* and several other genera in this family are partially parasitic. They produce their own food by photosynthesis, but also 'supplement their diet' by attaching their roots to those of adjacent plants, mostly grasses, thereby absorbing minerals and other nutrients. The leaves of Yellow Rattle are distinctly toothed.

The large and prominent calyx is flattened when flowering, but, when the seed capsule begins to develop, it inflates. Both stages are evident in the illustration. The bright yellow flowers, generally marked with purple on the upper lip, are adapted for pollination by bees and butterflies. The four stamens are enclosed in the upper lip. The anthers hang down and move. There is a fringe of hairs on the anthers, so that when they are touched by an insect the pollen falls directly upon it. There are two openings in the 'mouth' of the corolla: a narrow opening just below the stigma allows butterflies to insert their tongues and sip the nectar, and a wider opening further down allows shorter-tongued insects like bees to reach the nectar. In both cases, as the insect sips the nectar, it gets dusted with pollen, which it transfers to the stigma of the same or a different flower. The seeds have a wing around their equators, except where attached to the capsule, which helps to carry them on the wind.

Yellow Rattles, introduced from Europe, grow in fields, thickets, roadsides, and grassy headlands across Newfoundland and Labrador. They occur west to Alberta and south to Maine.

Baie Verte

Hemlock Parsley

Conioselinum chinense (L.) BSP
Parsley Family
Umbelliferae

The Hemlock Parsley is a dainty plant that looks too frail to survive on the headlands where it is often found. The compound name, *Conioselinum*, consists of the names of two other genera in this family which it resembles: *Conium*, Poison Hemlock, and *Selinum*, Milk Parsley. *Chinense* means of China, from where Linnaeus thought it originated.

The stem may be stout or slender depending upon the conditions under which it is growing. Most sections of the plant are hairless but there are fine, short hairs on parts of the inflorescence. The finely divided compound leaves grow in a basal rosette and also from the flowering stalk. All Umbelliferae have umbels. In this type of inflorescence, the stalks of a number of flowers are attached to the end of a common stalk and vary in length so that the flowers form a level surface. This plant has a compound umbel where a number of umbellets are attached to a common flower stalk. Each flower has an ovary with longitudinal ribs, and five white petals and five stamens attached to its top. There are no sepals. Although the flowers are individually small, they are conspicuous when arranged in an umbel. Insects readily land on the flat surface to sip the abundant nectar; their legs brush the anthers, transfer pollen, and effect pollination. The fruit consists of two halves that split apart at maturity.

This species grows in thickets and on headlands all over the island of Newfoundland and north to central Labrador. It occurs west to western Ontario and south to North Carolina. Another species, the Dwarf Hemlock Parsley (*Conioselinum pumilum* Rose), which is smaller, with purple leaf sheaths, grows on the serpentine barrens of the west coast of Newfoundland and in Labrador.

Bay d'Espoir

American Eyebright

Euphrasia americana Wettst.
Figwort Family
Scrophulariaceae

American Eyebright is a widely occurring plant and its various species bloom over a long season. Although the flowers are tiny, their intricate detail can be seen with careful examination. *Euphrasia*, Greek meaning cheerfulness, refers to its reputed value in improving eyesight in ancient times. *Americana* means American.

There are 10 species of *Euphrasia* throughout Newfoundland and Labrador, and, since they are similar, the following description will serve for all of them. They differ from each other and from the illustrated species, *Euphrasia americana*, in the bracts of the inflorescence, as well as flower size and structure. Most species branch. They vary in height from a few to almost 20 centimetres. The leaves, which have dark green and jagged edges, complement the flowers, and the purplish stems add to the overall colour contrast. The blossoms of some species are scattered along the stems, but, in American Eyebright, they are condensed into a head. The dainty, pretty flowers have a landing platform in the form of the lower lip; an insect's attention is drawn to the centre of the flower, the location of the nectar, by radiating mauve lines and a bright yellow 'eye.' If its earlier medicinal uses were not known, its common name, Eyebright, would suggest its bright yellow centre. Although insects visit these plants, they can effect self-pollination by bending back the style. The stigma then comes into contact with the anthers and is dusted with pollen.

American Eyebright is a common species on headlands along the coasts of the island of Newfoundland. It also occurs in southern Labrador, eastern Quebec, the Maritimes, and coastal Maine.

Baie Verte

Greenland Scurvygrass

Cochlearia groenlandica L.
Mustard Family
Cruciferae

This is one of the most dangerous plants to collect in Newfoundland and Labrador. The plant itself is harmless, but to reach where it grows on ledges and crumbling banks above the sea often requires foolhardy courage in the absence of mountain-climbing skill. *Cochlearia* is from *cochlear*, a spoon, which refers to the shape of the leaves in some species. *Groenlandica* means of Greenland.

Greenland Scurvygrass, a biennial, produces a rosette of somewhat fleshy leaves in its first growing season. During the second year it blooms and produces seeds for the next generation. The yellowed leaves of the first year's rosette are seen in the illustration. The roots have an interesting adaptation which equips them for growth on the crumbling banks mentioned above. If the roots are injured or the shoots destroyed, the roots have the capability of producing 'reparative' buds that grow into new plants. This is an unusual ability, but undoubtedly useful in a harsh and unstable environment.

The flowers and fruit are typical of members of this family. The four petals are in a cross-shaped pattern (thus the family name, Cruciferae), and, of its six stamens, there are four long ones in the centre and two shorter ones to the outside, a situation termed tetradynamous. The fruit are separated by walls. When the outer walls fall off to release the seeds, the central wall, which looks like a piece of glassine envelope stretched over a frame, is exposed. The seeds are attached to the frame. Honesty or Money Plant (*Lunaria*) has a larger version of this fruit.

This species is a halophyte. It grows in damp, saline soil along coastal areas of western, northern, and eastern Newfoundland, and on the coast of southern Labrador. It occurs throughout the arctic and Newfoundland is its southern limit on this continent.

Scurveygrass was a valuable herb used by early sailors to prevent scurvy, that great hazard afflicting early seamen. This plant tastes like watercress and can be used in a salad or sandwich.

Cape Bonavista

214

Roseroot

Sedum rosea (L.) Scop.
Orpine Family
Crassulaceae

Another common name for this plant is Live-forever, a description of its ability to survive for a long time. Plants collected to make dried botanical specimens often continue to put out new growth for months even though they have been squeezed between paper in the darkness of a plant press. *Sedum* is from *sedere*, to sit, and refers to the way that the plants perch on rocks and cliffs. *Rosea* refers to the fragrance of the roots when bruised. This species is also known as *Rhodiola rosea* L.

The root of Roseroot, which has a brown, flaky bark, can reach astonishing proportions. It penetrates small cracks and fissures in the rock and often forms most of its bulk on the surface of rock, where it presents a gnarled and weathered form. The numerous stems are thick and fleshy, as are the leaves. The leaf margin may be smooth or, more rarely, toothed. The whitish aspect of the leaves is the result of a layer of wax secreted onto the surface. The wax effectively sheds the droplets of salt spray which would otherwise destroy the leaves by dessicating them. This waxy coating is an essential adaptation for life on sea cliffs. Male and female flowers are borne on separate plants. The mass of male flowers look fluffy with their numerous long stamens (centre and right in illustration). The female flowers are in a prickly mass usually tinged with purple.

Roseroot grows mainly on the sea cliffs of the shores of Newfoundland and Labrador and extends along the Arctic Ocean and south to Maine.

The root of this succulent is reported to be tasty but astringent. In northern regions where greens are scarce, the young leaves and stems are added to salads and the stems and leaves used as greens until the flowers open.

Baie Verte

Pale Corydalis

Corydalis sempervirens (L.) Pers.
Fumitory Family
Fumariaceae

This Newfoundland and Labrador wildflower looks exotic with its dainty intricate flowers and its lacy leaves. *Corydalis* is the ancient Greek name for the crested lark. *Sempervirens* means evergreen, which it is not.

The greyish-green compound leaves of the Pale Corydalis complement its delicately coloured flowers. The pale colour of the leaves is due to small particles of wax produced by the leaf and deposited on the surface.

The flowers are worthy of careful examination: pick one, carefully pull the petals off with a straight pin, and hold the flower down with another to expose the stamens; examine the stamens with a magnifying lens to see two strap-like structures, each with three pollen sacs at the tips. This is a different arrangement from most plants. The nectar in the pouch of the flower attracts wasps and other insects to its blossom. In its efforts to sip the nectar, the insect usually effects pollination.

The Pale Corydalis is found in disturbed rocky areas in central Newfoundland and north to central Labrador. It ranges from Alaska, south to Montana and northern Georgia.

Baie Verte

Common Evening-primrose

Oenothera biennis L.
Evening-primrose Family
Onagraceae

This imposing plant is one of contrasts: it stands tall and straight, with coarse-looking seed capsules but delicate blossoms. *Oenothera* was used by Theophrastus for a species of *Epilobium* (fireweeds and willowherbs); it comes from the Greek meaning imbibing wine, presumably because a related European plant was thought to cause a thirst for wine. *Biennis* means biennial.

The Common Evening-primrose is a stout plant, a biennial that forms a rosette of fairly long leaves and strong fleshy roots during its first year. A flowering stem up to one metre tall grows during the second year. The stem, which is usually unbranched, is green (as illustrated) or purple-tinged and ranges from hairless to hairy. The flowers have their parts in fours and open in the evening, when they emit their perfume. This smell, and the pale colour, are characteristic of moth-pollinated flowers (other 'moth colours' are white and lavender). The flowers fade the next day. The seed capsules break open at the tips, and, as the plant sways in the wind, the seeds are thrown out. The seeds are long lived. In 1879 Dr. W.J. Beal of the University of Michigan buried the seeds of 21 species of common weeds in a special container. After 60 years, the seeds of only three species germinated, and Common Evening-primrose was one of those species. The last portion of the seeds will be tested in 2039.

This species grows throughout the island of Newfoundland in dry, open soil. Its range extends west to southeastern Alberta and south to northern Florida. There are two other species of Evening-primrose in this province, which are usually smaller.

The roots of this species can be eaten during their first winter. They must be gathered from late fall to early spring, and, after being cooked in two waters, taste somewhat like parsnips. If collected too early or too late, however, they have a sharp, peppery taste.

Grand Falls

Canada Thistle

Cirsium arvense (L.) Scop.
Daisy Family
Compositae

Cacti and thistles, which are prickly and quickly avoided, have flowers that seem fashioned from silk. *Cirsium*, from *cirsos* (a swollen vein), was a name given to these plants by Dioscorides, since thistles were reputed to be a remedy for swollen veins. *Arvense* means of fields.

Many species of thistle are biennial, but this one, with its extensive system of branched subterranean rhizomes, is perennial. The stems range from 50 centimetres to one metre in height and they have numerous leaves. The leaves are basically the same shape as those of dandelion, but are undulating and smooth or slightly woolly on the lower surface; the teeth end in sharp, rigid spines. Nettles have stinging hairs and cherries have a bitter tasting substance that discourages animals from browsing until the fruit is ripe, but the spines of Canada Thistle are particularly effective deterrents to grazing animals, and the wavy aspect of the leaf aims the armament of spines in all directions. The 'flowers' of this thistle are usually mauve, although a white-flowered form has been reported. The seeds are borne on the wind with the aid of their tufts of fine bristles. As this thistledown is soft and silky, fine things are often compared to it.

The Canada Thistle was introduced to North America from Europe and grows in cultivated and disturbed ground across the island of Newfoundland. There are three other species of *Cirsium* in Newfoundland but they look different from this one.

This plant can be eaten in the spring when it is young; however, the spines must be cut off the young leaves before steaming. Peel the young stems before boiling; they are reported to be tender and have a flavour like artichokes.

Baie Verte

Sheep Sorrel

Rumex acetosella L.
Buckwheat Family
Polygonaceae

This plant is a traditional nibble for children in Newfoundland and Labrador, many of whom know it by its common names, Sweet Leaf and Sally Suckers. *Rumex* is the ancient Latin name of dock, another species of this genus. *Acetosella*, little sorrel, is the old genus name for the sorrels.

Sheep Sorrel is a tenacious weed when it becomes established in gardens. It has an extensive root system and the ability to produce suckers. Sucker production is fairly common in shrubs and trees such as lilacs, poplars, and blueberries but uncommon in herbs. In attempting to remove this plant from a garden, small pieces of the rhizome often break off, and, before long, the plant is thriving once again. The presence of Sheep Sorrel in a plot of soil indicates that the ground has become sour (acidic) and an application of lime is needed. Lime improves soil and makes conditions unfavourable for this plant. The leaves of Sheep Sorrel have basal lobes that give it its hastate shape. The two stipules in this and other members of the family are fused into a papery sheath, an ocrea, which encircles the stem. The flowering stem rises as high as 30 centimetres and has an overall lumpy appearance. The flowers range from yellowish to reddish in colour. The numerous seeds are often grazed by cattle and other animals and dispersed by them as they pass through their digestive tracts.

Sheep Sorrel grows in fields and pastures all over Newfoundland, north to central Labrador, the rest of North America, and beyond. It has become naturalized from Europe. A similar species is the more robust Garden Sorrel (*Rumex acetosa* L.), which lacks the basal lobes on its leaves.

Sheep and Garden Sorrels were used as culinary herbs by the Egyptians, Greeks, and Romans, as well as medicinally as diuretics and for kidney stones. They were also used to improve the blood, and, since they contain iron, probably did. Horace recommended it for queasy stomachs, a common situation amongst a people devoted to Bacchus, the god of wine. The slightly acid taste of the plant makes it a pleasant addition to a salad, and it is also good as greens. Sorrel soup is famous in French cuisine. This plant, however, contains oxalic acid and should not be consumed in large quantities or too often.

Baie Verte

Hemp Nettle

Galeopsis tetrahit L.
Mint Family
Labiatae

This is a prickly little affair that makes weeding the garden unpleasant. *Galeopsis* is from the Greek *gale* meaning weasel and *opsis* meaning appearance. *Tetrahit* means four-parted.

The height of these annual plants varies considerably within the confines of a single garden. They range from an unbranched specimen about 10 centimetres to a branched monster of nearly one metre. The entire plant is covered with short, stiff hairs that deter browsing animals. The stem, which is square in cross-section, is swollen below each node, where the leaves attach. The calyx has five lobes that are elongated and sharply pointed which protect the entry to the developing seeds. The corollas are attractive: the upper lip is gracefully arched over the four stamens (two long and two short). The range of colour and patterns of the corolla is incredible, varying from almost pure mauve to pure white and considerable pattern variation in between. The illustration shows four seeds in a calyx, and the species name may refer to this feature.

Hemp Nettles are found in gardens, roadsides, and other disturbed sites all across Newfoundland and north to central Labrador. These natives of Eurasia have done well in the New World and are common weeds of the northern United States and Canada.

Baie Verte

Common St. John's-wort

Hypericum perforatum L.
St. John's-wort Family
Hypericaceae

In pre-Christian days in Europe this plant was dedicated to Baldur, the sun god, because it came into bloom around Midsummer's Day. When 24 June became St. John the Baptist's feast day, these yellow flowers were dedicated as St. John's herb or wort. This plant was hung in doorways and windows or carried as a safeguard against thunder and witches. *Hypericum* is Greek for over the heath and refers to the type of soil where it grows best. *Perforatum* means perforated.

This perennial herb can grow to one metre in height and branches considerably. The leaves are intriguing, since small transparent spots are observed when the leaf is held to the light. These spots mark the locations of large glands in the leaf that contain and secrete a colourless substance, hypericin, that causes photosensitization in animals. After eating St. John's-wort, animals develop what appears to be a severe case of sunburn, and death usually results. The flowers, with their bright yellow petals and numerous stamens, are typical of the family. The conical seed capsules contain numerous tiny seeds that germinate readily when dispersed.

Common St. John's-wort is found on the island of Newfoundland in waste grounds around communities. There are four other *Hypericum* species on the island, but they are small and grow in wet and boggy areas. Common St. John's-wort is naturalized from Europe and occurs west to British Columbia and south into Central America.

In addition to warding off thunder and witches, this species, when gathered on Midsummer's Eve, was a protection from imps, evil spirits, and the demons of melancholy. In Europe its juice was used to heal wounds, and in North America the Indians used this native species to heal wounds and to cure consumption.

Baie Verte

Lady's Thumb

Polygonum persicaria L.
Buckwheat Family
Polygonaceae

The elongated pink flower heads of Lady's Thumb brighten roadsides. *Polygonum* means many joints and refers to the places where the leaves attach to the stem. *Persicaria*, an old name for this plant, refers to a resemblance between the leaves of this species and those of the peach (*Persica*).

Lady's Thumb grows in clumps and may rise to a height of 40 centimetres. The bright green leaves have a purplish thumbprint in the centre of the blade. The two stipules of this plant and of other species in this genus are fused into a tube at the base of the leaf. This structure, an ocrea, sheaths the stem. The flowers are pink or, very rarely, white. The black shining seeds may be two- or three-angled on the same plant. Charles Darwin, the first to study the transport of seeds in mud on the feet of birds that frequented the water's edge, found the seeds of rushes, sedges, *Polygonum*, and aquatic grasses in mud from their feet. As seeds can be carried in mud on the feet of animals and people and on the wheels of vehicles, it is evident why Lady's Thumb occurs where it does.

Lady's Thumb, which was introduced from Europe, grows in damp places, cultivated ground, roadsides, and disturbed sites all across Newfoundland, except the Northern Peninsula, in central Labrador, and across North America.

Baie Verte

Blue-eyed Grass

Sisyrinchium bermudianum L.
Iris Family
Iridaceae

Blue-eyed Grass is an appropriate common name for this plant which many people invite to their gardens. *Sisyrinchium* was a plant name used by Theophrastus, an ancient Greek philosopher, and *bermudianum* means of Bermuda. Linnaeus described a specimen of this plant from Virginia and another plant from Bermuda. Through some confusion, Blue-eyed Grass, which was found in Virginia, received the wrong name. This species does, however, grow in Bermuda.

At first glance, the bluish leaves look grass-like, but a closer examination reveals that they are arranged in fans like those of *Iris*. The flowering stalk is terminated by two sheathing leaves from which the flowers emerge one at a time. The seed capsules are attractively coloured and dangle gracefully like little marbles on fine wire.

There is only one species of Blue-eyed Grass in Newfoundland and Labrador and it grows in moist spots in various habitats. The distribution of Blue-eyed Grass is fascinating. It is found across the United States and southern Canada. In addition, it is found at Goose Bay, Labrador; southwest Greenland; and in Counties Galway and Kerry, Ireland.

This plant makes a charming addition to a flower border or rock garden. It does not like to be crowded, so plant it on its own.

Baie Verte

Field Sowthistle

Sonchus arvensis L.
Daisy Family
Compositae

The climate and soils of Newfoundland and Labrador have their advantages and disadvantages. The Field Sowthistle is a cosmopolitan weed that can be troublesome, but, on the island, it is just another pretty wildflower. *Sonchus* is the ancient Greek name for these plants. *Arvensis* means of cultivated ground.

The roots of this perennial species extend deep into the ground as well as horizontally. They can send up shoots everywhere around the main plant, and pulling up the plants does not eradicate them. The somewhat fleshy leaves are prickly along their margins but not as much as the true thistles. The bases of the leaves have lobes that clasp the stem. The prickles provide the stem with extra protection from grazing animals.

The 'flowers,' which consist solely of ray florets, resemble Dandelions. The styles bear two stigmas that spread outwards (see illustration). Cross-pollination is favoured, and these outstretched stigmas pick up pollen from visiting insects. Should this not occur, the tips curl under and come in contact with the anthers, thus effecting self-pollination. The spindle-shaped seeds have a fine parachute of slender bristles that carry them over long distances. These seeds have prominent ribs and tiny lumps all over them.

Field Sowthistles are not common but they do grow in fields, and on roadsides, gravel beaches, and various disturbed sites all over the island of Newfoundland. They also occur west to Alaska and throughout the northern United States. In Newfoundland, there are also two annual species that have much smaller flowers.

They taste bitter in the same way as Dandelion, but Field Sowthistles are used as greens in the early spring.

Dildo Run Provincial Park

234

Common Speedwell

Veronica officinalis L.
Figwort Family
Scrophulariaceae

Common Speedwell is one of the first colonizers of gravel patches and leads the way in beautifying these areas. *Veronica* is named for St. Veronica and *officinalis* means of the apothecary shops.

The opposite leaves and trailing stems of this plant are covered with little hairs that make it appear greyish. The spikes of flowers arch gracefully upwards. The blue of the flowers is not particularly bright but it is eye-catching since it seems to stand out subtly from the grey of the rocks. The flowers of this and other *Veronica* species show a reduction in the number of parts compared with other members of the family. The petals are fused into a tube at their bases but are separate for most of their length. There are normally five petals in other members of the family, but in *Veronica* two of the petals have fused along one edge, so it looks as if there are only four petals. The stamens are attached to the petal tube at their bases, and, instead of the usual five stamens of the family, there are only two in *Veronica* species. The seed capsule is hairy and heart-shaped.

Common Speedwell has been introduced from Europe and grows in gravel areas, open woods, fields, and any other area where it is fairly dry and there is not too much competition from other plants. Newfoundland and Labrador has 11 other species of *Veronica* with which this one can be confused. Common Speedwell occurs across the island of Newfoundland, except for the Northern Peninsula, and as far west as Ontario and south to Tennessee.

Common Speedwell has been used to make tea; however, it is better mixed with other tea herbs. Steep; do not boil.

Baie Verte

Field Pennycress

Thlaspi arvense L.
Mustard Family
Cruciferae

In early autumn Field Pennycress plants, with their plumes of green pennies, stand out in a field or roadside. *Thlaspi* is from the Greek *thlaein*, to crush, referring to the flat fruit. *Arvense* means of cultivated ground.

The Field Pennycress is hairless and shiny. The leaves have auricles ('ears') at their bases, which clasp the stem. The flowers are small but the fruit are a good size. Some plants avoid pollination with cleistogamy, whereby flowers are produced but do not open. Self-pollination occurs in the closed bud and fruit are produced. Cleistogamy occurs routinely in some plants, but in many it is triggered by such environmental conditions as submersion in water, drought, cold, excessive heat, and shade. In *Thlaspi*, cold is the trigger. Most seeds are released from the seed capsule while the capsule is attached to the plant. To aid dispersal, the seeds of some species are flat and blown by the wind, but, in *Thlaspi*, the entire fruit detaches, is blown by the wind, and the seeds are released when the fruit lands.

This species grows along roadsides, waste places, and fields across the island of Newfoundland and north to central Labrador. It was introduced from Europe and occurs across much of North America. In places it is a weed of grain fields.

The young leaves can be eaten as greens and the seeds used like mustard seeds.

Baie Verte

Fall Dandelion

Leontodon autumnalis L.
Daisy Family
Compositae

This is the last of the dandelion-like plants to bloom each year in Newfoundland and Labrador. These spots of sunshine brighten the places where they grow until late into autumn. *Leontodon* is from the Greek *leon* meaning a lion and *odous* meaning tooth, referring to the pointed teeth along the edges of the leaves. *Autumnalis* means autumnal.

A stout stem at the surface of the soil has thick fibrous roots growing downwards, and numerous leaves in a crown above. The size of the entire plant depends upon its environment. The range in size is so great that it often requires a second look to ascertain that a plant is the Fall Dandelion. The leaves are deeply toothed and have scattered hairs on the surface. The flowering stalks branch and range from 10 to 30 centimetres in height. Although they are slender, they are surprisingly resilient and can withstand strong winds and physical abuse from trampling feet. The normal sort of 'flower' is illustrated, but another form, *ochroleuca*, has plump, pale greenish-yellow 'flowers' with no ray florets, which may be caused by a disease or some aspect of the environment. The seeds are equipped with a parachute for dispersal by the wind, but studies have shown that they can withstand a trip through the digestive tract of grazing animals and be dispersed in this manner.

Fall Dandelions are natives of Europe and like most immigrants they are doing well in the New World. They grow in fields, on roadsides, and in other disturbed habitats all over Newfoundland and north to central Labrador, blooming throughout much of summer and fall. They also occur west to western Ontario and south to Pennsylvania. Although they resemble a number of other plants, its rosette of distinctive leaves and branching flowering stalk should allow easy identification.

Baie Verte

241

Orange Hawkweed

Hieracium aurantiacum L.
Daisy Family
Compositae

According to Greek folklore, hawks used the juice of Hawkweed to sharpen their eyesight. In medieval times the Orange Hawkweed grown in gardens in England was called 'Grim the Collier' because of the sooty black hairs on the flower buds and stalks. *Hieracium* is from the Greek *hierax* meaning hawk and *aurantiacum* means orange-coloured.

The basal rosette of leaves is usually large and sends out numerous stolons to form new plants. The whole plant is covered with fairly long white hairs, and, in the region of the flowers, there are numerous black hairs. The flowers are delightful. The production of seeds in this species is fascinating since it can occur in various ways. Upon germination, embryos, which are protected in the seeds, develop into seedlings and are normally formed after an egg and sperm have united in the process of fertilization. This occurs occasionally in this plant. It also forms embryos from cells that surround the egg and these are duplicates of the plant. This is a form of cloning and leads to large numbers of almost identical plants in one locality.

Orange Hawkweed, a native of Europe, is found around settlements on the Avalon Peninsula, and central and western Newfoundland. It grows on roadsides, clearings, and pastures. It is particularly abundant in Clarke's Beach, Conception Bay, where it literally carpets acres within the town's boundaries; it is not particularly abundant outside of this settlement. It occurs west to Minnesota and south to Virginia. Although attractive, it and other species of *Hieracium* can be troublesome weeds since they form large mats that crowd out grasses and other plants eaten by livestock. This has earned *Hieracium* species the common names of Devil's Bit, King Devil, and Devil's Paintbrush.

Tilt Cove

Common Dandelion

Taraxacum officinale Weber
Daisy Family
Compositae

The cosmopolitan Common Dandelion exhibits remarkable powers to defy eradication of its gold from the green carpets around our dwellings. *Taraxacum* is from *Tharakhchakon*, the Arabic name for the plant. *Officinale* means of the apothecary shops and refers to its extensive use in medicine during the Middle Ages.

A plant's distribution tells much about its success as an organism. The Common Dandelion occurs worldwide. It has many mechanisms for successfully competing with other plants and for producing and dispersing seeds. Individual plants can be seriously damaged by animals and people, yet they can regenerate if even a small piece of root is left in the ground. Dandelions attract insect pollinators by producing relatively large quantities of nectar and abundant pollen. While the weather is often cool in the spring when they flower, and insects may be scarce, viable seeds can be formed by apomixis, a process that does not involve pollination and fertilization. Seeds are therefore produced despite adverse conditions. The seeds carry a 'parachute,' which is a highly effective method of dispersal. Dandelion seeds can be carried vast distances in the jet stream, and pilots have sighted them at remarkable altitudes. Dandelion seeds have grapnels at the top to catch on the soil when the seed settles to the ground and germinates.

Common Dandelion is found in lawns, pastures, and disturbed areas everywhere on the island of Newfoundland and north to central Labrador. It was introduced to the New World from Europe. Five other species of Dandelion grow on the island and are found more commonly in alpine and coastal sites.

This species has been used as a tonic for centuries. It was especially valuable during the Middle Ages, when its rich store of vitamins and minerals supplemented the diet in the late winter and early spring. It is an excellent source of calcium, potassium, and vitamin A. Dandelion leaves, crowns, and flower buds can be used in salads or as greens in the spring. Boil twice and sprinkle with fried bacon or olive oil. The flowers are used for making wine, and the roots are roasted and used as a coffee substitute.

Baie Verte

Hedge Bindweed

Convolvulus sepium L.
Morning-glory Family
Convolvulaceae

These flowery trumpets are a joy to find since there are so few large single flowers in the boreal region. It is little wonder that they have been used so much in fanciful illustrations of fairy tales. *Convolvulus* is from *convolvere* which means to entwine, and *sepium* means of hedges.

The stem, with its lance-shaped leaves, entwines itself around any object it encounters – stumps, trees, fences, or other such supports. It grows to a surprising length each summer and branches freely. Each flower has two large leafy bracts at its base. There are five sepals, and the five petals are fused into the trumpet-shaped corolla, which may be pure white, particularly in the St. John's area, or pink and white as illustrated. Architects have borrowed from this plant for some of their designs: a pillar shaped like the corolla of this plant can support a large area above on a small area below. The globe-shaped seed capsule contains four seeds.

Hedge Bindweed occurs in certain localities across the island of Newfoundland, but does not reach the Northern Peninsula.

As this plant is reported to cause illness in pigs, avoid giving it to domestic animals.

Connaigre Bay

Bull Thistle

Cirsium vulgare (Savi) Tenore
Daisy Family
Compositae

The imposing Bull Thistle commands respect. *Cirsium* is from *cirsos*, a swollen vein, for which the thistle was once used as a remedy. *Vulgare* means common.

This biennial herb produces a large rosette of prickly leaves during the first year and a flowering plant in the second year. The plant is usually less than one metre in height and has several stems, but tall plants of over one metre with a single stem and several side branches are sometimes found in the same area. The entire plant is spiny, which serves as a protection against browsing animals. The stem is woody and ridged with a fine cobweb covering of hairs. The upper branches have spiny wings and often the leaves have a spiny wing that continues down the stem. Each segment of a leaf ends in a long stout spine and has shorter spines along the margins. These spines, combined with the convoluted nature of the leaf, make the plant impregnable.

The flower is typical of the Daisy Family in that it is not a single flower but an inflorescence consisting of many small florets. The purple florets protrude from the spiny cup of bracts that protect them. The seeds are equipped with a parachute of fine hairs that help disperse them on the wind.

This species originally came from Europe and the Middle East with early colonizers. It is a fairly common weed around communities throughout North America. On the island of Newfoundland, it is found around larger settlements and ports, where it grows along roadsides, in pastures, and in disturbed sites.

Disarmed, Bull Thistle is edible. The young parts of the plant are collected in the early spring, the spines cut from the leaves, and the young stems peeled and cooked in salted water for a few minutes and served as a vegetable.

Nipper's Harbour

Common Tansy

Tanacetum vulgare Nutt.
Daisy Family
Compositae

The Common Tansy, with its yellow buttons and strongly fragrant leaves, has been a familiar plant since it was brought to North America by early European settlers. Tansy comes from the French *tanesie* and that comes from the Greek *athanasia*, which means immortality. This may have been suggested by Common Tansy's long-lived scent and its medicinal uses. In the Middle Ages, it was placed around a corpse in a coffin for the wake. The origin of *Tanacetum* is uncertain, and *vulgare* means common.

The long stout rhizomes anchor the plant. The stem is about one metre tall with finely divided leaves. The strong odour is produced by a volatile oil carried in a system of ducts that run parallel to the 'veins' (xylem and phloem) in the stems, roots, and leaves. Various functions have been suggested for this oil, but the most likely is that it discourages tiny organisms from entering and damaging the plant. The 'flowers' are one-half to one centimetre broad and consist entirely of disc florets, although ray florets may be present.

The Common Tansy is found around communities across the island of Newfoundland, but not on the Northern Peninsula. It also occurs across Canada and the United States.

A tea was brewed from Common Tansy in the Victorian era and there was much debate as to whether the "perfectly vile-tasting" fluid was worse than the rheumatism, measles, and other ailments it treated.

Grand Falls

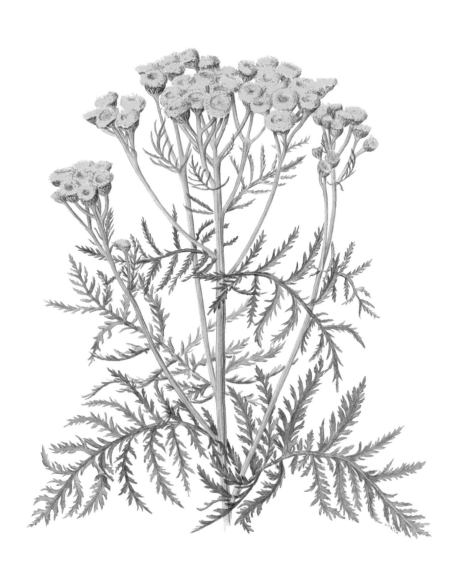

Heal-all

Prunella vulgaris L.
Mint Family
Labiatae

This is a charming plant with 'spruce cones' from which the flowers protrude. The origin of *Prunella* is unknown, and *vulgaris* means common.

Heal-all is a simple plant. It is usually unbranched, although it may have one or two pairs of branches from the base, and it only has about three or four pairs of leaves. The entire plant is covered with small, stiff hairs. The 'spruce cones' mentioned above consist of broad bract-like leaves that overlap and are closely packed into a short spike. Three flowers associated with each of these leaves protrude when they are ready to open. The corollas, which vary in colour from bluish, violet, or lavender to white, have the upper and lower lips typical of the Mint Family. These flowers are especially adapted to pollination by bees. The fruit consists of four nutlets, which remain in the calyx until they are mature.

This species is found widely throughout the Northern Hemisphere. It grows on most of the island Newfoundland except the Northern Peninsula and north to central Labrador, in disturbed areas and roadsides, but it is especially common in pastures and grasslands where sheep and other domestic animals graze. It was introduced from Europe and has now become naturalized.

The other common name for Heal-all is Carpenterweed or *Herbe au Charpentier*. Presumably this plant was used for healing purposes in the past and, possibly, by carpenters.

Lewisporte

Coltsfoot

Tussilago farfara L.
Daisy Family
Compositae

Coltsfoot is the first uncultivated spring flower to bloom on the island of Newfoundland. It adds a cheery note to the prolonged transition from winter to summer and announces the coming of spring when it seems that winter will never end. *Tussilago* is from the Latin, *tussis*, a cough, for which it has been a remedy for thousands of years. *Farfara* means coltsfoot.

The rhizome of Coltsfoot, which sends up flowers and then leaves, can be extensive, as any gardener can attest. The first Coltsfoot blooms often open in late March in the St. John's area. The flower stalks have reddish scales along their length; the flower looks something like a Dandelion, but its rays are much narrower. The leaves appear in late spring and give the plant its common name. They are supposed to resemble the outline of a colt's foot. The young developing leaves have a dense covering of hairs on both surfaces that protects the delicate tissue until a waxy coat is deposited on the upper surface. At maturity the leaf only has hairs on its lower surface.

This species, which grows around towns and settlements on the island of Newfoundland, was introduced from Europe. It extends west to Minnesota and south to New Jersey. It is one of the first of the dandelion-like flowers in Newfoundland to bloom each year. Coltsfoot is followed by Dandelion (*Taraxacum officinale* Weber), Hawkweeds (*Hieracium* spp.), and Fall Dandelion (*Leontodon autumnalis* L.).

Coltsfoot has been used since the time of the early Greeks to treat respiratory ailments. As Coltfoot has a pleasant flavour, the leaves can be used to make cough drops or syrup and dried to steep as a tea. The leaf is also a chief component in herbal tobaccos. It can be smoked by itself for coughs and wheezes or mixed with thyme, peppermint, dried rose petals, and other fragrant herbs. For centuries, Coltsfoot and Dandelion have been widely used herbal medicines.

Corner Brook

Bering Sea Chickweed

Cerastium beeringianum C & S
Pink Family
Caryophyllaceae

Chickens enjoy eating this and other chickweed species. I used to feed my flock great mats of Bering Sea Chickweed every morning and the plant pigments made the yolks a deep, rich yellow. *Cerastium* is from the Greek *cerastes*, horned, which refers to the shape of the seed capsule. *Beeringianum* means of the Bering Sea.

The plant forms a mat of hairy stems and leaves. Glandular hairs on the stems can be seen by holding the plant up to a light. *Cerastium* species are usually called Mouse-ear Chickweeds because of the fuzzy, rounded leaves. Each petal is lobed so that at first glance there appears to be 10 petals. The seed capsule opens, just at the tip, by valvate dehiscence. The seeds are flung out when the stems thrash about in the wind.

This species occurs on roadsides and open gravelly areas across Newfoundland and Labrador, across boreal North America, and in northeastern Asia.

Baie Verte

Black Knapweed

Centaurea nigra L.
Daisy Family
Compositae

If lumps of dark green plants are evident in a well-grazed pasture, it is probably Black Knapweed. Animals carefully avoid it. *Centaurea* is from *Centaurie*, an ancient Greek name for a plant associated with the mythical Centaur. *Nigra* means black.

Black Knapweed is a coarse plant with tough stems and leaves. The entire plant feels rough. It can grow up to about 80 centimetres in height. The attractive flowers, which are in fact a cluster of florets, resemble thistle flowers. Plants are not generally thought to move very much, but several parts of the Black Knapweed flower do. The stamens are designed so that they ensure the dispersal of pollen to the flowers of other plants of the same species. The stamens spread outwards when the flowers are open, but as soon as they are disturbed, by an insect for example, they contract and bend inwards. The pollen is tipped onto the visiting insect, which then carries it to another flower.

When the seeds are mature and ready to disperse, they are protected from leaving at the wrong time. The florets of this composite flower are surrounded by fringed dark brown phyllaries. The phyllaries curl inwards when the air is damp and outwards in dry air. This prevents the seeds, which are dispersed by the wind, from being released during rainy weather. On the island of Newfoundland this species has difficulty producing seeds, because a small fly lays its eggs in the flowers. The larvae hatch and eat the young seeds and then overwinter within the phyllaries. Birds subsequently visit the flowers during the winter and eat the larvae, thereby establishing a food chain centred on the Black Knapweed.

Black Knapweed is not as attractive as its relative, the Bachelor's Button or Cornflower (*Centaurea cyanus* L.), but it is lovely along roadsides and in fields. It was introduced from Europe and is now found on the Avalon Peninsula, in the Corner Brook area, and near St. Anthony. It also grows as far west as Ontario and south to Virginia. Black Knapweed has become a serious pest of grazing lands in some areas of North America. It has not been reported to be poisonous, but animals seem to avoid it.

Baie Verte

Rough-stemmed Goldenrod

Solidago rugosa Ait.
Daisy Family
Compositae

Cultivated varieties of Goldenrod grow in England and Europe, but in North America it is a roadside plant. Its mounds of butter-yellow in the late summer and autumn are glorious and as beautiful as many garden favourites. *Solidago* is from the Latin *solidus*, whole, and probably refers to its once-reputed qualities for healing wounds. *Rugosa* means rough-stemmed.

Most goldenrods of this type form dense clumps of stiff, upright, rod-like stems. The stems of this species have stiff hairs. The plants are generally about 65 centimetres tall, but they may reach over one metre. The sharp teeth along the margins of the leaves are distinct and widely spaced; and the leaves have one prominent vein. The 'flowers' are attached all around the branches of the inflorescence, but their stalks are bent so that they all face upwards. The seeds are covered with short hairs.

The Rough-stemmed Goldenrod grows in clearings, along roadsides, and in other disturbed habitats all across the island of Newfoundland, but is absent from the Northern Peninsula. There are seven species on the island and three in Labrador. It also occurs west to Saskatchewan and south to Texas and Virginia.

Baie Verte

Yarrow

Achillea millefolium L.
Daisy Family
Compositae

Yarrow and Dandelion are so plentiful in temperate regions and elsewhere that they are often overlooked as too common to notice. The plant on the roadside, however, is just as pretty as the illustration. *Achillea* is named for Achilles, and *millefolium*, which means thousand-leafed, refers to the finely dissected leaves.

The entire plant contains aromatic oil that is released when the plant is bruised. These plants have a stout, creeping rhizome that branches. The stem is usually not branched except in the inflorescence and the entire plant can vary from almost hairless to hairy. The leaves are of a compound type known as bipinnatifid: pinnatifid leaf blades are deeply divided, but there is still some blade tissue left along the midrib. In a bipinnatifid leaf, each segment is again divided – thus twice-divided. The fine divisions and the crisped nature of the leaf make it look like thousands of little leaves. All of the 'flowers' form a flat-topped cluster. Each 'flower' consists of outer ray florets with their broad corolla segments and a group of disc florets in the centre. The rays are typically white but they can be different shades of pink (a pale form is illustrated).

Yarrow is naturalized from Europe and grows in fields, roadsides, and other disturbed habitats throughout the island of Newfoundland, north to central Labrador, and across North America. It is circumboreal in distribution. Yarrow, as a species, shows tremendous variation and some botanists recognize a number of species and others only this one.

Baie Verte

262

Tansy Ragwort

Senecio jacobaea L.
Daisy Family
Compositae

Tansy Ragwort is a pretty wildflower that brightens roadsides with golden yellow in late summer. It is not as well liked in other parts of its range where it is highly invasive. *Senecio* is from the Latin *senex*, an old man, and refers to the hairiness of some species. *Jacobaea* means of St. James as it blooms on St. James' Day (25 July).

The rootstalk is stout, and the tall stems, bearing lobed, wavy leaves, rise from it in a clump. The flat head of flowers is usually abuzz with visiting insects. Each plant produces many seeds, which furthers its spread in an area. It produces persistent rosettes of leaves on golf courses and elsewhere. It is classed as a noxious weed. Fresh and dry leaves are dangerous to livestock; when consumed over time, they damage the liver and can lead to death.

This species is native to Europe, Asia Minor, and across Asia to Siberia. The plant, which is now found across North America, is thought to have spread after being introduced to Pictou, Nova Scotia, around 1850.

St. John's

Common Groundsel

Senecio vulgaris L.
Daisy Family
Compositae

Common Groundsel is an easily overlooked common weed, with an interesting and long association. Groundsel is thought to be derived from an Old English word meaning ground swallower. It is an enthusiastic member of a garden's vegetation. *Senecio* is from the Latin *senex*, meaning old man, and refers to the hairiness of some species and the white hairs of the pappus in this and other species. *Vulgaris* means common.

This is one of three similar species. It has no ray florets and the phyllaries are black-tipped; the other two species have minute ray florets and the phyllaries are not black-tipped. The Woodland Groundsel (*Senecio sylvaticus* L.) is slightly hairy, while the Stinking Groundsel (*Senecio viscosus* L.) is covered with sticky glandular hairs. The fruit, which are often thought of as seeds, have a tuft of hairs on the top. This pappus is considered to be modified sepals. It helps bear the fruit aloft and can travel about 40 kilometres.

This species is native to Eurasia and grows in cultivated land, waste places, and roadsides across North America. It occurs across the island of Newfoundland and in Labrador north to Hopedale.

In the first century Pliny recommended Common Groundsel as a salve for toothaches. In the Middle Ages it was mixed with wine to cure stomach aches, and in the twenty-first century it is sometimes added to herbal lotions for eyes and chapped hands. The seeds of Common Groundsel are a component of canary seed mixes.

Baie Verte

Butter-and-Eggs

Linaria vulgaris Hill
Figwort Family
Scrophulariaceae

One of two weedy scourges that can afflict a garden is Butter-and-Eggs; the other is Sheep Sorrel (*Rumex acetosella* L.). Both of these plants spread by subterranean rhizomes and an entire crop of these weeds can spring from tiny fragments left in the soil after weeding. *Linaria* is from *Linum*, the flax, and refers to the similarity of their leaves. *Vulgaris* means common.

The crowded leaves of this plant are a whitish-green and contrast well with the flowers, which are similar in appearance to those of their cousin, the snapdragon. The upper and lower lips form the entrance to an exclusive drinking club. The flower is mainly butter-yellow with a contrasting egg-yolk-orange spot on the lower lip, which attracts the attention of insects. They land on this spot and, if they are heavy enough, the lip drops and they sip the nectar from a spur that protrudes from the back of the flower. The anthers and stigma are placed so that only an insect of a particular size can effect pollination. This special gate excludes small insects that would only steal nectar. The top-shaped seed capsules have one gaping opening from which the winged seeds are released. If the flowers are not pollinated, or if the plant is growing in too much shade, then the plant can form cleistogamous flowers that do not open but do produce seeds. The stamens elongate so that the anthers are next to the stigma, and pollen is released onto it. Cleistogamous flowers also occur on other plants such as violets (*Viola* spp.) and sundews (*Drosera* spp.). In this way seeds are produced even under unfavourable conditions.

Butter-and-Eggs was introduced to North America from Europe. It occurs all across the island of Newfoundland, but particularly along roadsides and around settlements. There are two other *Linaria* species: Striped Toadflax is white with purple stripes, and Hedge Toadflax, which is considered to be a hybrid of Striped Toadflax and Butter-and-Eggs.

Baie Verte

269

Striped Toadflax

Linaria repens (L.) Mill.
Figwort Family
Scrophulariaceae

The common name, Striped Toadflax, is descriptive of this plant. The purple striping of the flower is apparent and the flax part refers to the resemblance of the stem and leaves to those of flax. The flower resembles a toad's mouth, much as a snapdragon resembles a dragon's mouth. *Linaria* is from *Linum*, flax, and *repens* means creeping.

The underground rhizome of this plant creeps extensively under the soil, sending up numerous branching stems. The entire plant suggests laxity: the stems straggle, the narrow leaves are scattered along the stem, and the flowers are in a lax spike and usually only a few open at a time. The flowers resemble miniature snapdragons and have a conical nectar sac protruding from the back of the corolla. A small yellow spot on the lower lip directs the attention of any visiting insects to the place where they can gain access to the nectar. Only insects heavy enough to push down the lower lip can sip nectar and effect pollination in the process. The seed capsules contain three-sided seeds.

Striped Toadflax is a native of Europe that has become naturalized in a few localities of eastern North America. It is found on the Avalon Peninsula, in Corner Brook, and a few other locations. It occurs in scattered sites south to eastern Pennsylvania. It grows along roadsides, and in fields and other disturbed areas on the island of Newfoundland. There are two other species on the island – Butter-and-Eggs (*Linaria vulgaris* Hill) and Hedge Toadflax (*Linaria sepium* Allman). Butter-and-Eggs is yellow, and Hedge Toadflax, thought to be a hybrid, is intermediate.

This species brightens roadsides and other areas. During the Middle Ages in Europe, it was used to treat jaundice, piles, and conjunctivitis, and, boiled in milk, it made a fly poison.

St. John's

Cow Vetch

Vicia cracca L.
Pea Family
Leguminosae

The rich colour of these flowers adds a royal touch to roadsides and fences as Cow Vetch scrambles up grass and wire to thrust its flowers upwards. *Vicia* is the ancient Latin name for these plants and *cracca* the species. The Italians call Cow Vetch *Cracca*, and the French call it *Vesce craque*.

Cow Vetch can grow to over one metre in height. It has an angular stem and compound leaves. The leaflets have fine hairs on their surfaces, and the tips are rounded, with hair-like projections. This plant clambers up over other plants, fences, stumps, and other objects by means of tendrils which are actually modified leaflets. The terminal one to three leaflets do not develop blades but instead become coiled tendrils that wrap themselves around any object they encounter. The inflorescence consists of many small mauve flowers that become blue-violet as they fade. This contrast of colour, as well as the concentration of the flowers on one side of the stalk, attracts insect pollinators. Bees tend to land on the lowest flowers of an inflorescence and work their way upwards.

Members of the Pea Family have complicated flowers and a careful study of an actual flower is needed to fully understand the structure. Of the five petals, the two lower petals, which are fused along one edge, envelop the stamens and pistil and are called the keel. The two lateral petals are called the wings and in this species they are fused to the keel. The upper petal is called the standard. There are 10 stamens: the uppermost is separated, but the filaments of the other nine are fused into a tube with only the anthers separate. The anthers surround the club-shaped stigma, which is covered with many fine hairs. When an insect lands on one of these flowers, it usually settles on the wings. They separate under the weight and the keel is pushed downwards. The exposed stamens dust the insect's abdomen, and pollen from another flower which may still be adhering to the insect is dusted onto the hairy stigma.

Cow Vetch is found across the island of Newfoundland and north to central Labrador in fields, open areas, and roadsides. It was introduced from Europe and occurs west to British Columbia and south to Virginia. There are three other species of vetch in this province, but they do not have such a large inflorescence.

Baie Verte

273

Meadowsweet

Spiraea latifolia (Ait.) Borkh.
Rose Family
Rosaceae

This delightful shrub is interesting in both summer and winter. The dainty flowers enhance many a summer's scene and the cinnamon-coloured seed capsules are attractive in the winter. *Spiraea* is from the Greek, *speira*, meaning wreath, and *latifolia* means broad-leafed.

Meadowsweet forms clumps about 50 centimetres in height but it can grow to over one metre. The woody branches are reddish-brown and, on the older stems, the bark tends to shred. The leaves are broad, as the species name suggests, and in the autumn they turn a peachy-yellow. Most flowers have white petals but some have pink (both are illustrated). The pollination mechanism in this genus is effective in ensuring seed production. When the flower is in the bud stage, the stamens are bent towards the centre, and the stigmas, which project beyond the stamens, are receptive to pollen even before the flower opens. After the flower opens, the stamens gradually become erect and the outer ones shed their pollen first. Insects are attracted to the flowers by the abundant nectar secreted by an orange-yellow nectary that surrounds the ovaries. Insects pollinate the flowers, but, as a final resort, pollen can fall from the innermost stamens onto the stigma. The numerous small seeds are borne in the five small tubular seed capsules.

This species is found along roadsides, and in meadows, fields, and other open habitats across the island of Newfoundland, but it does not extend up the Northern Peninsula. It occurs west to Michigan and south to North Carolina.

Meadowsweet is a good candidate for gardens and makes an attractive low hedge where exotic species would not do as well.

Bay d'Espoir

Red Clover

Trifolium pratense L.
Pea Family
Leguminosae

This is a strikingly handsome plant with attractive leaves and a flower cluster that glows when lit by the sun. *Trifolium* refers to the three leaflets of each leaf and *pratense* means of meadows.

Red Clover grows in clumps up to 50 centimetres in height, and the stems are finely hairy. Each leaf is attached by a stalk that has a broad, triangular stipule on each side at its point of attachment to the stem. Each leaflet has a whitish marking shaped like an arrowhead that enhances the appearance of the plant as a whole. The flowers are crowded into a head at the end of the flowering stalk, with several leafy bracts at the base of the head. The flowers are not attached by stalks; rather, they are attached directly to the flowering stalk by the base of the calyx.

The flowers are intricate in structure. The corolla consists of five petals fused at their bases. There is an upper petal (standard), two fused into a boat-like structure which encloses the stamens and pistil (keel), and two lower petals (wings). Ten stamens surround the pistil. Nine filaments are fused into an almost-complete tube and the tenth filament is separate. When a bee visits the flower, it lands on the two lower petals. These are attached to the boat-like structure and the whole is depressed to expose the enclosed sexual organs. The stigma comes into contact with the insect, which is usually well dusted with pollen from previous flowers, as it sips the nectar in the flower. When the pollinating insect flies off, the boat-like keel springs back to cover the stamens and pistil.

This species grows across the island Newfoundland and north to central Labrador in meadows and clearings, and along roadsides. It also occurs west to British Columbia and south into Central America. Now naturalized on this continent, Red Clover came from Europe. There are five species of clover in Newfoundland and Labrador. Alsike Clover (*Trifolium hybridum* L.) has pinkish flowers, each attached by a distinct stalk. Hop Clover (*Trifolium agrarium* L.) has yellow flowers; and White Clover (*Trifolium repens* L.) is the common white-flowered clover of lawns, the real culprit behind 'grass' stains on clothes.

The flowers, dried or fresh, of Red and other clovers make a refreshing tea on a hot day. The young shoots can be eaten as greens.

Baie Verte

277

Ox-eye Daisy

Chrysanthemum leucanthemum L.
Daisy Family
Compositae

"She loves me; she loves me not . . ." – how simple it is to determine if he or she is an object of affection. The Ox-eye Daisy has served countless generations of youths well. *Chrysanthemum* is from the Greek for yellow flower and *leucanthemum*, which was the old genus name, is Greek for white flower.

The Ox-eye Daisy can grow as tall as 70 centimetres. The leaves have ragged margins and vary considerably in overall shape from the base to the tip of the stem. The flower is typical of the family and illustrates the benefit of this arrangement. The yellow disc florets contrast well with the white ray florets, so that insect pollinators are attracted to land. They sip nectar and as they move about on the centre of the flower, pollen is transferred from the anthers to the stigmas by their feet. Slugs have been observed to creep across the flower during damp weather and they presumably also effect pollination.

This species is widespread on the island of Newfoundland and north to central Labrador, and throughout North America. It was introduced from Europe and it grows in fields and waste places and along roadsides. Several types of chamomiles on the island of Newfoundland bear similar flowers, but, compared with the Ox-eye Daisy, their leaves are finely divided.

In addition to the romantic use mentioned above, the young leaves of this plant can also be used for salads. The flavour may be too pronounced for some people, but a taste may be acquired.

Baie Verte

Pearly Everlasting

Anaphalis margaritacea (L.) Clarke
Daisy Family
Compositae

Pearly Everlasting is a visitor from Asia that seems to find conditions in Newfoundland and Labrador to its liking, but it has not become a nuisance. *Anaphalis* is derived from *Gnaphalium*, a genus in which it was first placed, and *margaritacea* means pearly.

The stems arise from a creeping rhizome that roots along its length. The first leaves that unfold in the spring are densely woolly with abundant white hairs. As the stem develops and elongates, the first leaves wither. The leaves of the stem are long and narrow and the margins are rolled under. The upper surface tends to have fewer hairs than the lower. The flowers are composite flowers, as there are several florets enclosed by the pearly-white phyllaries, which are similar in texture to those of the strawflower. They feel like straw and, as the common name suggests, they last for a long time. The seeds have tufts of hairs that act like parachutes in a breeze and carry the seeds over a considerable distance.

The Pearly Everlasting is found along roadsides, in disturbed sites, and in gravelly soils across the island of Newfoundland and north to eastern Labrador. It also occurs in the northern half of the United States and throughout much of Canada.

This species is inedible, but it is attractive in winter bouquets. Pick the whole stem just before any of the flowers begin to show yellow florets. Strip off the leaves and hang the plant upside down in a cool, airy place until it is dry. It can then be used with other dried plant material in a perpetual flower arrangement.

Baie Verte

GLOSSARY

Alternate Leaves – leaves attached singly at different heights on the stem, e.g., rose and aster.

Anther – the pollen-bearing portion of the stamen that is borne on the tip of the filament.

Apogamy – a form of apomixis where an embryo is produced without the usual fertilization of an egg by a sperm.

Apomixis – the process by which a seed is produced without fertilization.

Auricle – an ear-shaped appendage, usually at the base of leaves or petals.

Berry – this term is used generally in this book to refer to a fleshy or juicy fruit.

Bipinnatifid – refers to a compound leaf. The leaf is divided into leaflets and the leaflets again are divided, e.g., yarrow.

Boreal – refers to northern regions, e.g., the coniferous forest regions that stretch across Canada, Asia, and northern Europe.

Bract – a small leaf that may be scale-like, associated with flowers, e.g., Lesser Rattlesnake Plantain and Crackerberry.

Calcareous Soil – soil with a relatively high amount of limestone.

Calyculus – a 'second' calyx consisting of a whorl of bracts, e.g., Three-toothed Cinquefoil and Common Strawberry.

Calyx – collective term for sepals. It is used in this book to refer to sepals that are fused edge to edge at their bases or for much of their length.

Capitulum – the inflorescence of the Daisy Family (Compositae). The tiny flowers (florets) are crowded together into a head.

Capsule – this term is used in a general way to refer to fruit that are dry and have a brittle wall.

Chlorophyll – a green pigment in plants that captures the energy of the sun's rays in the process of photosynthesis.

Cleistogamous Flowers – flowers that do not open, but produce their fruit by self-pollination in the bud. These are usually formed when weather conditions are poor, e.g., violets and Butter-and-Eggs.

Compound Leaf – a leaf that has two or more leaflets, e.g., Virginian Rose and Cow Vetch.

Corolla – collective term for the petals. It is used in this book to refer to petals that are fused edge-to-edge at their bases or for much of their length.

Coniferous – refers to evergreen trees that bear cones, e.g., spruce and fir.

Cross-pollination – the transfer of pollen from the flower of one plant to the stigma of a flower on another plant of the same species, by such agents as insects and wind.

Deciduous – woody plants that shed their leaves in the autumn.

Dehiscence – the splitting open of a seed pod or anther.

Drupe/Drupelet – a fleshy fruit that has the seed enclosed in a stony pit, e.g., cherry, and peach. Raspberry fruit is an aggregation of drupelets.

Embryo – the tiny plant contained in the seed.

Epicotyl – part of the embryo in the seed which develops into the shoot with its stems and leaves.

283

Epipetalous – refers to the stamens that are attached to the corolla.

Falls – a special term applied to the petals of iris flowers that droop down.

Fertilization – the fusion of an egg and sperm that follows pollination and results in the production of a seed.

Floret – the individual flowers that make up the composite 'flowers' of the Daisy Family.

Fruit – the fleshy or dry seed-bearing structure that develops from the ovary after pollination.

Genus (pl. Genera) – a group of closely related species, e.g., Cypripedium is a genus of which three species are described in this book.

Germinate – a seed germinates or sprouts when the embryo grows into a seedling.

Glabrous – without hairs.

Gland – a structure that produces a fluid.

Glandular Hair – a hair with a bulbous gland on the tip, e.g., Skunk Currant.

Gynostemium – the 'column' or central structure in an orchid flower that is formed by the fusion of the stamens, style, and stigma.

Halophyte – a plant that grows in a salty soil, such as sea beaches and salt marshes.

Hastate – leaves shaped like an arrowhead.

Hypocotyl – the part of the embryo in the seed that develops into a root system.

Inferior Ovary – an ovary that has the sepals and petals attached to the top, e.g., Fireweed and Small Purple Fringed Orchid.

Inflorescence – a grouping of two or more flowers.

Involucre – one or more whorls of bracts (phyllaries) at the base of a capitulum in the Daisy Family (Compositae).

Keel – two petals of a legume flower, united along one edge and enclosing the stamens and pistil.

Leaflet – a section of a compound leaf.

Lenticel – a pore in the bark of some woody plants.

Ligule – the strap-like corolla of the ray florets of a capitulum.

Monocot – one of the two groups of flowering plants characterized by one seed leaf, parallel veins in the leaves, and flower parts in threes or multiples of threes.

Mycorrhiza – an association of a fungus with the root of a plant, thought to be beneficial to both.

Nectar – a sugary fluid produced in a flower to attract insects, birds, and other pollinators.

Nectary – a gland in a flower that produces nectar.

Node – a joint of the stem, bearing a leaf or leaves.

Oblanceolate – the leaf is lance-shaped with the broader part of the blade towards the tip rather than the base.

Ocrea – a special structure of the leaves in the Buckwheat Family (Polygonaceae). It is a sheath at the base of the leaf, formed by the fusion of the two stipules.

Opposite Leaves – two leaves borne at a node on opposite sides of the stem, e.g., Turtlehead and mint.

Ovary – the lower portion of the pistil that contains the ovules.

Ovule – contains the eggs that develop into seeds after fertilization.

Palisade Cells – located in a layer just below the surface of the leaf. They contain a large concentration of chlorophyll and are where most of the photosynthesis occurs.

Parasite – a plant that obtains its nutrition from another plant.

Petal – found inside the sepals in the flowers and is usually brightly coloured.

Petiole – the stalk of the leaf.

Phloem – the portion of the veins that carries the food manufactured by photosynthesis from the leaves to other parts of the plant.

Photosynthesis – the process by which organic material (glucose) is produced from water and carbon dioxide using energy absorbed by chlorophyll from sunlight. Oxygen is another product of photosynthesis.

Phyllaries – bracts which surround the florets in the flowers of the Daisy Family (Compositae). Collectively, they make up an involucre, e.g., New York Aster and Fall Dandelion.

Pinnate – a compound leaf in which the leaflets are attached along the leaf stalk (rachis), e.g., rose and dogberry leaves.

Pistil – the female part of the flower, consisting of the ovary, style, and stigma.

Pollen – sperm-containing grains produced in the anthers.

Pollination – the act of transfer of pollen from an anther to a stigma.

Resupination – the flower opens upside down as a result of the twisting of the flower stalk or ovary (in orchids).

Rhizome – an underground stem that differs from a root in that it has nodes, buds, or scale-like leaves, e.g., Wild Calla and Wild Lily-of-the-Valley.

Scale – small leaves or bracts that are dry and pressed to the surface.

Scape – a leafless stalk arising from a rosette of leaves and bearing one or more flowers.

Self-pollination – the transfer of pollen from the flower of one plant to the stigma of a flower on the same plant.

Sepal – one of the parts of a calyx. It is usually green and serves to protect the flower as it develops before it opens.

Silique – the special fruit of the Mustard Family (Cruciferae), e.g., Greenland Scurvygrass.

Spadix – the thick, fleshy inflorescence found in the Arum Family (Araceae).

Spathe – the bract surrounding the spadix in the Arum Family (Araceae).

Spur – a sac-like projection of a sepal or petal that contains a nectary, e.g., Spotted Touch-Me-Not and Northern White Violet.

Stamen – the male part of the flower, which consists of a filament (stalk) and the pollen-producing anther.

Staminode – a stamen that does not produce pollen and usually lacks the anther, e.g., Turtlehead.

Standard – the broad, upper petal of a legume flower or the erect petals of an iris.

Stigma – the tip of the pistil that gets sticky and receives the pollen.

Stipule – a small leaf-like structure or a scale found in pairs at the base of a petiole or sepal.

Stolon – a shoot with a long stem that gives rise to a new plant at its tip, e.g., Strawberry and Orange Hawkweed.

Style – the stalk above the ovary that has the stigma on its tip.

Succulent – a juicy or fleshy plant.

Syngynium (pl. syngynia) – union of the ovaries of two flowers. This occurs in honeysuckles (Lonicera).

Taproot – a type of root system that has a large main root growing downwards and smaller lateral roots, e.g., Dandelion and carrot.

Tepals – when the calyx and corolla (sepals and petals) are not differentiated, the segments are called tepals, e.g., iris.

Tetrads – a group of four. The pollen grains of the Blueberry Family (Ericaceae) are shed in groups of four rather than singly.

Tetradynamous – an arrangement of stamens characteristic of the Mustard Family (Cruciferae), four stamens in the centre and two shorter ones on the outside of the group.

Toothed – when the margin of a leaf is ragged, with tooth-like projections.

Trichomes – plant hairs, of many lengths and shapes.

Valvate – sections of a seed capsule that has split open (dehisced).

Veins – the vessels which conduct water, nutrients, and manufactured food in the stems, leaves, and roots.

Whorled Leaves – three or more leaves at a node in a circle, e.g., Joe-Pye-Weed.

Xylem – the portion of the veins that carries water and dissolved nutrients from the roots to the leaves.

Wildflowers Index

Peter J. Scott is curator of the Agnes Marion Ayre Herbarium and a professor in the department of biology of Memorial University of Newfoundland. His research interests include flora of the province of Newfoundland and Labrador, plant ecology, and biotechnology. He is also a gardening commentator for radio and television programs.

Originally from Saskatchewan, **Dorothy Black** is a graduate of the University of British Columbia. She moved to Baie Verte, Newfoundland and Labrador, with her physician husband in 1965, where they and their three children lived until 1980. During her last five summers there, she painted wildflowers in watercolour, traveling with her family to communities throughout the province in a motor home. She now pursues her art in eastern Ontario.